England's Dances

FOLK-DANCING
TO-DAY AND YESTERDAY

☆

A brief account of the Folk-Dances of England, of their possible origin and of the present movement to restore them to the English people

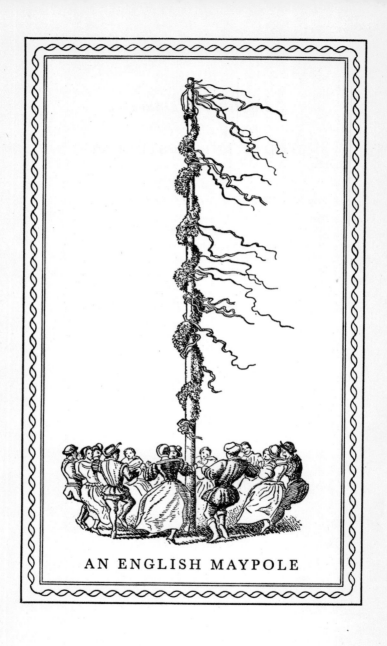

AN ENGLISH MAYPOLE

England's Dances

FOLK-DANCING TO-DAY AND YESTERDAY

☆

Douglas Kennedy

DIRECTOR OF THE
ENGLISH FOLK DANCE
AND SONG SOCIETY

London
G. Bell & Sons, Ltd
1950

First published 1949
Reprinted .   . 1950

PRINTED IN GREAT BRITAIN BY RICHARD CLAY AND COMPANY, LTD.,
BUNGAY, SUFFOLK.

To My Dancing Partner

Contents

The Illustrations

Introduction

by

DR. R. VAUGHAN WILLIAMS, O.M.

ALL traditional art was originally applied art, and as
Mr. Kennedy tells us, primitive dancing was an accompaniment to religious ritual. The ritual has dis-
appeared. Ought the dancing to remain? Yes, on
one condition—that it has the elements of beauty and
vitality.

This is the faith of the English Folk Dance and
Song Society.

In this book you will learn from Mr. Kennedy how
to preserve our English dances in all their beauty; but
preservation is not enough, as he will tell you. The
dances must not be treated as museum pieces and put
in a glass case. They must have vitality as well as
beauty. We must let the fresh air of progress blow on
them.

This will involve development and perhaps even
change. Each generation will, rightly, react to these
dances in a different manner.

It has been said that traditional art is an individual
flowering on a common stem. By all means let us encourage the individual flowering, but we must not lose
touch with the common stem. Above all, let us treat
our dances as things of beauty, then I firmly believe
that they will be a joy for ever.

Preface

DANCING is the oldest of the arts. It has its origins in the animal world and its roots are buried deep down in human nature. Long before it became an art, dancing figured as a ritual in tribal custom and primitive religion. From the ancient rituals of the past are descended the Folk-Dances of to-day. Any study of their origin involves reference to the story of mankind as a whole.

The English are fortunate in the variety of types of dance that have been preserved. They were unfortunate in the extent of the damage done to country life and hence to village custom by the spread of industrialism.

Our knowledge of our national dance tradition, which we owe mainly to the work of Cecil Sharp, has, since his death nearly a quarter of a century ago, been extended by investigators in this and other countries, and by reference to similar folk customs in many parts of the world. Even so, the story remains dim and somewhat confused.

In writing this brief outline of it, the author approached his task with little qualification other than his dancing and teaching experience. He is painfully aware of the dangers of the over-simplification inevitable in an endeavour to make the picture clear to the 'ordinary reader', who, he hopes, will forgive such simplification for its own sake. The expert and scholarly readers will at least sympathise with the difficulties, even if they deplore certain omissions and disagree with some of the theory.

I would like to thank my friends who have helped me, and particularly my wife, to whom the book is dedicated. Especially would I like to acknowledge my debt to my secretary, Prudence Muirhead, who prepared and corrected the typescript.

D. N. K.

I

Discovery and Revival

ENGLISH country life had by the early 19th century evolved a finely balanced rural economy and a harmonious relation of landlord, tenant and worker which depended on the certain demand for home-produced food. With the advent of foreign, imported food, the old economy broke down and rural workers were driven to seek new forms of employment in the new towns. Townsfolk, losing interest in country products, lost interest in the countryside itself, and in the lives of those who worked there.

Foreign imports were not confined to cheap food. Everything that came from abroad was more fashionable than the home-made article. To foreign art and artists the doors were opened wide. Music was no exception. To be a successful professional musician it was necessary to adopt a foreign name. There could be no good English music. As for native music, the Scots and Irish had their songs, of course, but the English—they had none. In the neglected countryside many ancient local customs persisted, but some faltered and some died completely. Many of the country folk tenaciously, almost secretly, clung to old ways and continued among themselves to sing their old songs and dance their old dances.

Towards the end of the century, several musicians

in different parts of England, attracted by the quality of the music they heard sung by the country people, published collections of the local country songs. But little was done to record the local folk-dances, and it was not until Cecil Sharp, himself a folk-song collector, chanced to see at Headington, Oxford, a group of Morris dancers on Boxing Day, 1899, that the English folk-dance caught the attention of its preordained recorder. Cecil Sharp was deeply impressed with the vigour and the beauty of the Morris Dance tunes that he heard and noted on that day, but it was not until some years after that he was moved to collect the Morris Dances themselves, and to introduce them to the public. The musician of the Headington team, William Kimber, was very ready to lend a hand, and to give Sharp the benefit of the Kimber family knowledge of the dances and their music. Kimber first taught the collector how to dance the steps and then helped him to describe the movements. Cecil Sharp's subsequent career as a folk-dance authority is now well known. His life has been written, and his published books of Morris Dances, Sword Dances and Country Dances have been the main source of information on the English traditional dances for the last thirty-five years. William Kimber still lives at Headington, and regards himself, rightly, as the father of the folk-dance revival in England.

It was this revival which occupied the remainder of Sharp's life and which eventually wore down his frail constitution. From 1906, when he published his first folk-dance book, until his death in 1924, he never paused from teaching, lecturing and proselytising, except to collect more dances and tunes. His first essay in presenting the Morris Dance to the public was somewhat fortuitous. He had been engaged in teaching his recently collected folk-songs to the members of a working-girls' club. Revelling in this new experience, they asked him if he could find some dances to match. This request reminded him of the Morris Dances, so he brought William Kimber up from Headington, and together they started to teach the girls. They performed the Morris with a lively vitality, though naturally much of its essential character was missing. But when the performers began, in their turn, to teach, the results bore still less relation to the Oxfordshire original that had captivated Sharp. Dissatisfied with this first essay, he then looked round for a source of reliable teachers, and for a centre where he could conduct experiments on the various dances he was collecting. He found what he wanted at a physical-training college, and succeeded eventually in raising a mobile demonstration team of men and women who, under his personal guidance, could dance well enough to illustrate his lectures. At this time (December, 1911), with a nucleus of enthusiasts who had formed a Folk-Dance Club, he founded the organisation designed to carry on the work of arousing public interest in the newly recovered dances. This was the English Folk-Dance Society, and my first introduction to the organisation of which Sharp was appointed the Honorary Director.

Up to the outbreak of the first World War, this Society, through its Honorary Director, established dance-groups in various parts of the country and organised Holiday Courses at Stratford-upon-Avon. With his team of demonstrators Sharp visited all the main provincial centres, and by 1914 there was already a considerable degree of public interest aroused as a direct result of his individual effort. By that time there was an available repertory of over a hundred Morris Dances, about twenty-five Sword Dances and several hundred Country Dances. During the 1914–1918 war Sharp visited the United States, and not only created interest in this new field of folk-music, but was himself plunged like the discoverer of a new land into the unsuspected richness of the English folk tradition in America. He spent several months in 1916 and 1918, assisted by Miss Maud Karpeles, collecting folk-songs in the Southern Appalachian Mountains.

At the end of the war, when Sharp returned to England, he found that the public response to folk-dancing was increasing. There was now a wide demand for instruction in the dances, especially from school teachers of all kinds. The number of school teachers, mostly women, since the men were away in the Forces, had increased considerably during the war. The Board of Education which had advocated Morris Dancing in the schools in 1909 and wished to encourage it as far as possible, appointed Cecil Sharp to visit training colleges, and Helen Kennedy to visit schools, to stimulate the practice of traditional dances, songs and games among children.

From 1919 until 1924 this educational work, together with the growth of the Society in other directions, occupied practically the whole of Sharp's time. He continued to publish songs and dances, including a large number of country dances which he had transcribed from John Playford's 17th-century collection. The American–English songs that he had collected in

2. A Mediaeval Chain Dance or Carol, showing Animal-Men and a May-Bush.

3 Children watching a Punch and Judy Show:
a spontaneous Morris Dance.

the Appalachian Mountains ultimately exerted a great influence in the United States, and to Sharp is due a great deal of the credit for the widespread interest in American folk-music that has grown up in the United States during the last twenty-five years. Sharp himself, were he alive to-day, would be astonished to find the neglected songs and tunes he collected in Kentucky and Tennessee, now being featured in films and heard in dance-halls in the great metropolitan capitals. Even so, before he died, Sharp said of himself that it was given to few pioneers to see so much fruit of their labours within their lifetime.

Towards the end of his life Sharp had already begun to realise that too much emphasis had been laid on the educational aspect of folk-dancing. He was seeking to adjust this bias by judging at folk-dance festivals and, indeed, at any gatherings where he had opportunity to address the public. He hoped ultimately to shift the folk-dance away from the classroom back to its proper festival setting. The opportunity to demonstrate how this ought to be done was not granted him in time. When he died, the Society launched an appeal for a memorial in his name, and after five years the building was erected in Regent's Park which bears his name and houses the headquarters of the Society he founded. His death, far from discouraging his followers, gave a great impetus to the folk-dance revival, and although a few of his personal friends thought that public interest would wane after the pioneer had left the scene, in fact growth in membership of the Society went on steadily and support for the movement continued unabated.

Sharp's personal direction was succeeded by a triumvirate, Dr. Ralph Vaughan Williams, Miss

B

Maud Karpeles and myself. I was later appointed Organising Director.

We three proceeded to carry on Sharp's policy, and to follow the trail he had blazed. Gradually new elements were introduced into the working programme. An annual festival of folk-dance was given at the Albert Hall in London. Groups of traditional dancers in other European countries, and Societies working on similar lines, were invited to these festivals. At least one foreign team figured in the festival programme each year. English teams were often invited to perform abroad, and they visited most of the European countries as well as Canada and the United States during the next ten years. In 1935 an International Festival of Folk Dancers was held in London. This focused public attention vividly upon the traditional dances still alive in Europe, and also emphasised the wealth of the folk-dance tradition in England. The Society suffered a hang-over, however, from its early teething days, and a large section of the public continued to associate folk-dancing solely with school children and with new movements such as Women's Institutes and Girl Guides that had sprung up prior to the war and were growing rapidly into important national organisations.

When Sharp began his work of revival, he had started with the Morris Dance, a men's dance of vitality and vigour, but unsuitable as a form of social recreation. The first few Country Dances he published were social folk-dances collected directly from country people. His attention was then deflected to earlier collections of Country Dances preserved in printed books of the 17th and 18th centuries. Transcribing from John Playford's collection, 'The English Dancing Master', printed in 1650, he selected a number of examples which, with their lovely tunes, he considered could be adapted to popular use and to educational purposes. These found a place in his second book of Country Dances, the first being devoted to the traditional social dances he had collected directly from the country people. This new volume of period Country Dances was subsequently followed by further volumes as he worked his way through the various later editions of Playford's manual. It was these selected 17th- and 18th-century dances which Sharp offered to the public as the most suitable for social and recreational purposes. They were danced at parties by the members of the Folk Dance Society; they were taught in colleges and schools and in various other organisations. There was no doubt that these dances transcribed from Playford's manual had a very great appeal, both from the standpoint of the music and the construction of the dance formation, often highly elaborate and ingenious. But they did not lend themselves so readily to popular use, as did the simpler traditional Country Dances.

After Sharp's death it was gradually realised by those in charge of the Society's practical affairs that these traditional Country Dances should not have been supplanted by the 17th-century models. Steps were therefore taken to collect and encourage the surviving local Country Dances and to include an increasing proportion of these in the dance programmes used at social gatherings. An incident which happened during the visit of an English team to a North European Folk-Dance Festival at Copenhagen in 1929 served to drive home the need for this adjustment. After the English team had given its usual programme, a number of Scandinavian dancers first congratulated the English on their dancing, but then dumbfounded them by asking if England had no ordinary folk-dances? 'Your Country Dances', they said, 'are regular little ballets'. They were referring, of course, to the Playford Country Dances which had formed part of the English programme. A further incentive to give priority to the traditional Country Dances came from Canada and the United States, where so many of the English social dances have been found in current use and re-imported into the English repertory. Cecil Sharp himself, when song-collecting in the Southern Appalachian Mountains, had noted, and subsequently published in England, a form of the local 'Square Dance' which he called 'The Kentucky Running Set'. He justified its incorporation among the English folk-dances as being probably of English folk origin. There are many examples of the 'Square Dance' in other parts of the U.S.A., and this type of dance, with its particular technique depending upon a leader continuously calling the order of the figures, was taking root in this country before the recent war. By 1939 the Society was beginning to give priority to the traditional dance for social recreational use, and to reserve the Playford Country Dances for more specialised groups and purposes, but further progress of this development was postponed by world events.

When war broke out in 1939, the popular revival which Cecil Sharp had launched thirty years before could be fairly judged as only a partial success. Although millions of children must have learnt at least several of the Playford Country Dances, only a very small percentage of them continued folk-dancing after leaving school. The general public had not appreciably been touched: a small proportion were sympathetic to the idea of keeping alive the ancient traditions of dance and music, but more were actually prejudiced against it, and its practice was linked in the minds of many with the crank or with women and children. That there was a place in social recreation for a type of simple community dance was clearly demonstrated on many public occasions. The Jubilee, the Coronation and other national festivals where large crowds assembled were conspicuous for the instinctive but blind attempts of the crowds to form into dancing circles and to celebrate together. In the ball-room from time to time attempts have been made to create dances that would embrace the isolated couples, and some of these have become widely popular. The 'Palais Glide', the 'Conga', the 'Big Apple', 'Underneath the Spreading Chestnut Tree', the 'Lambeth Walk', the 'Hokey Cokey'—all have found some acceptance in the private and public dance-hall. One reason why the English folk-dance revival had not been able to administer to this hunger was that its material, the Playford Country Dance, was too complicated. It needed more detailed instruction and careful practice than the ordinary person, especially the ordinary man, was prepared to stand. The way out of that *impasse* lay in the simpler traditional dances, and in the American method of 'calling' so that the 'man in the street' could join in a set dance and lose himself in the crowd without having to ask the way. The American Square Dance, with its calling, had been introduced to English dancers a year or two before the recent war broke out. At first it was merely regarded as a novelty. Only gradually was it appreciated how readily this folk-dance lends itself to modern usage. In the Society's gatherings it was just establishing itself, alongside the English and other American traditional Country Dances, when war broke out, and further growth in the folk-dance revival ceased for the next six years.

During the war the revival marked time. The technical staff which the Society had trained, numbering nearly one hundred, left their Branch Societies for war work. From time to time the Society had received some measure of financial help from the Trusts and from Government sources. Government aid stopped with the outbreak of war, but the Pilgrim Trust, and later the Arts Council and the Carnegie United Kingdom Trust, continued to assist the Society through its war-time difficulties.

Towards the end of the war the governing committee took the opportunity to review and revise its policy in the light of past experience, and to plan the Society upon a national basis. A new constitution was approved and adopted in December, 1945 : the Ministry of Education offered to renew its financial support, and a new phase in the English folk-dance revival began.

All this time the revival of folk-dancing in England was having its repercussions in the United States, which, in turn, exercised some influence on the English revival. There are certain States where English traditions and connections are valued highly. Visitors from these States to Cecil Sharp's courses at Stratford-upon-Avon, strongly impressed with the folk-dances and tunes, were determined to import them. Some of these visitors were aware of the existence of American

Country Dances, but they felt sure that the 'Old Country' must have the best, and that America must have them, too. How much of Old England's music lay hidden in New England and other American States was yet to be revealed.

Soon after the English Society was formed (1912) there came a request from America for a teacher to go out and instruct college students and others in the 'new' English folk-dances, particularly in the men's dances. A member of Sharp's demonstration team agreed to accept this invitation, and he created enthusiasm wherever he went by his own magnificent dancing. Sharp was next asked to arrange for a teacher to go out and practise in the States. This led to the formation of a Branch of the English Society in Boston that has continued as an active centre of folk-dancing for the last thirty years. Then came the visit of Cecil Sharp himself. He and Maud Karpeles taught the dances to groups far and wide, when they were not hunting songs. In 1917 they published the first collection of 323 American folk-songs, all of British origin, and many of them probably derived from some part of England.

Sharp's discovery of the American–English folk-songs in the Southern Appalachian Mountains undoubtedly stirred the deep interest of many Americans. To them this discovery was a complete eye-opener. By a curious coincidence, while Sharp was song collecting in the Southern Appalachians, an American pioneer was simultaneously, but independently, prospecting this treasure ground of English folk-music. John Lomax was spared to continue this work of recording folk-tunes until his death in January, 1948, in his eighty-first year. Sharp and Lomax, the English and American pioneers, have left a lasting heritage for the peoples of both countries.

The growth of interest in American folk-dancing has perhaps been more gradual. The formation of the Branch of the Society in Boston was soon followed by other Branches, including one in New York City. This link between the American and English folk-dancers has been of real benefit to the revival. The music and dance traditions, common to the two peoples, are shared with freedom and great cordiality. Those English ritual dances, the men's Morris and Sword customs, which, if they were ever transplanted, never took root in America, have for many years been widely taught in the States. At the annual summer school of the Country Dance Society, Inc., held at Long Pond Camp, near Plymouth, Massachusetts, the English Morris may be seen performed by our cousins as featly as in England. The Flamborough Sword Dance could be danced by many an American College team. The English Country Dances are now so mixed with their American variants that it is often hard to know which is which.

In Cecil Sharp House, London, is a room named after Helen Storrow, who helped to build the Cecil Sharp memorial, and who created the Long Pond Camp in Massachusetts. The 'Running Set', from Kentucky, or the 'Green Mountain Volunteer', from Vermont, may be seen in a London Youth Club danced by Cockneys. But America's greatest contribution in the national exchange of folk-dance is 'Square Dance', with its caller and its fertile rhymes of reminder. It has a story of its own. (See Chapter VIII.)

II

Primitive Dance

In England, although it would be generally agreed that it is a good thing so much of our native dance and music tradition survived into the industrial age, there has been wide disagreement over the attempt to revive these traditions. Some have taken the view that England's folk-dances, being old and probably decadent, should be allowed to die a natural death. Cecil Sharp himself held that the dances were old, but they were so old that their actual age was a matter of indifference. The significant fact to him was that they expressed an element of eternity. He and his supporters argued that folk-dancing was the one form of dance which was completely natural, and its practice could only be beneficial. The weakness of this argument is that most human beings to-day are unnatural; that their mentality is no longer suited to the simplicity of the old country customs. Perhaps a more effective argument for the retention of our native traditions is that they save us the trouble of inventing them all over again. The primeval jigging of the Morris dancer provides both a tonic and an outlet, the need for which has driven young people of Europe and America to re-discover the 'jitter' and the 'jive'. While man continues to inherit something of his animal psychology and physiology, he will continue to find health and satisfaction in elemental dance. That other aspect of the folk-dance—the linking up of individuals into a group—is needed as much to-day as in the Middle Ages. At every social gathering, and on all occasions of civic celebration, there are blind attempts to create some community dance form. It would seem rather senseless to try to invent something that has been invented time and time again in the past. There already exist so many forms of community dancing that I believe it is no longer even possible for a dance-composer to produce something entirely new. While we continue to yearn to jig, as well as to get together, there is surely a place for the dances and dance-music that we have inherited from our own people.

Before giving an account of the different types of dance, I propose to discuss the probable origins of these types.

Our English word 'dance' is derived from the Low German 'tanz', but our word has a much wider application. The German word signifies to leap, stamp and hop about, and describes the actions of the individual. The nearest English equivalents of 'tanz', with its restricted meaning, are the words 'jig' and 'jitter': the latter perhaps conveying more vividly the primitive type of bodily action which is but one aspect of our conception of 'dance'.

The other type of dancing not defined by such brief words as 'tanz' and 'jig' has no longer any common English label to describe its nature. It had its own word in Mediæval England, but that word has long since been put to quite a different use. The lost word for this other 'dance' is the familiar 'carol', now restricted to describe a Christmas song. When it was said that the English carolled ('Angli jubilant'), the implication was that our national habit was to dance in the form of a linked-up chain, singing our dance-song as we wove through the winding maze of the dance. This picture of a group of dancers linked in a chain, threading a pattern, is a very different conception from that of a solo dancer jigging or jittering. Both conceptions now find a place in our single word 'dance', and the two contrasted actions have, in the course of our dance-history, each affected the other. There is no question as to which is the more primitive form of dance. In fact, one can fairly assume that the animal ancestors of man indulged in the jig, and that, when man emerged as something distinct from the rest of the animal world, he was, in the 'jig' sense, already a dancer. Naturalists, accustomed to observe the behaviour of certain animals, birds and insects, have made frequent references to antics which they describe as dancing. Birds, particularly, seem to have developed their own forms of the art, right up to the point of our concept of ballet. Dances which appear to belong to the ritual of courting are practised by male birds even when the female is absent. Birds have an advantage over the most skilful human dancer in that their wings provide them with a natural 'balon'. Bird-dances are perhaps too developed to reveal their primitive origin, but this can be traced in the antics of fledglings and, indeed, in the young of many other creatures. Everybody is familiar with the skip of the lamb and the caper of the kid. The young creatures appear to receive an electric shock that shoots them into the air and keeps them bouncing up and down several times before the impulse is spent. Their gambols look quite unpremeditated, and each young animal gives a startled look, as if to say 'I wonder where that came from?' The bounce springs from an accumulation of the surplus energy so plentifully supplied to growing creatures. The way in which this surplus is accumulated and then expended in an impulse or series of impulses, is characteristic of all organic life. There is little doubt that the effect on the organism is, on the whole, pleasurable, that there is a tendency to continue the impulse, at first spontaneous, into a wilful series of leaps. Having once been lofted, the little animal grows more aware of the pull of gravity and finds sheer joy in leaping against the pull and in turning the succession of rises and drops into a jig. Horses and dogs clearly enjoy this little play with gravity. The monkey, hanging on to the bars of his cage, gets such satisfaction out of the jitter he can set up in his cage that his bar-dance is a regular feature of his acrobatic routine.

And so we might expect to see, in the dances of primitive man, the same elemental jig forming the basis of a dance technique. The jumps and stamps vary in detail, but the rhythm of the up-and-down dances that go on for hours, and even for days, is a rhythm tapped out on the surface of the ground by the alternating rise and drop of the human body, like a drumstick on the stretched drumhead.

The dance of primitive man, once established as a habit, must have exercised an impressive influence upon his developing mentality, for dancing not only figures in practically every primitive culture that has been studied, but also finds a place in all the great civilisations. At some point in his early reactions to the pull of gravity he discovered the potency of rhythm. That power has continued to exercise an influence on human affairs that seems, at first sight, out of all proportion to the apparently insignificant nature of the first dance steps.

First of all, let me try to describe the direct effect on the individual of his own dance. The jig that alternately lifts him up and drops him down imparts a throbbing vibration felt in the solar plexus, and travelling outwards from that region to the extremities of the limbs. This is not a difficult process to imagine, if one pictures the excited antics of a small child who had just heard or seen something to delight him. Jumping off both feet and rippling the arms up and down as if to dash some drops of water from the finger-tips, the excited young primitive expresses pleasure in an impulsive jig. The rhythm that undulates up and down may be continued at will. It is a powerful function of rhythm that the mood which first induced it can be captured and recaptured by exactly repeating the rhythm: that is to say, invoker and invoked are interchangeable. It will be at once appreciated that here we have a useful control to enable man to condition his own mood. Why this should be so is not easy to explain, but an explanation of a sort is suggested if one remembers that the whole process of organic functioning, including the extremely complicated organism known as man, is based upon the rhythmical impulse. The healing properties of massage, or the encouragement of a lover's caress, and the response which this evokes, is due to the rhythmical, or musical, nature of the living substance. Every dancer, primitive or civilised, is aware of the exhilarating effect of his dancing, and of the almost incredible way in which the parts of his body and the facets of his personality tend to fall into harmony through the compelling influence of rhythm. But this internal effect of rhythm on the individual, while of great significance, is not so important for my present argument as the external effect exerted upon other individuals. This point is not so obvious for the civilised person to appreciate, at any rate in terms of dancing. Among primitives, however, dancing can arouse mass action and devotion as readily as did Hitler's emotional appeals. The rhythmic messages transmitted to a group of primitives by dancing, distilled and dispensed the potent medicine of the witch-doctor and Headman all through the stages of pre-history, right into modern times. Adventitious aids of every kind were introduced to help the medicine-man to convey his rhythmic messages: colour, sound, symbolic shapes and other properties can be recruited to emphasise the vital meaning. Let me reconstruct for you an imaginary incident in a hunting tribe. Let us assume a shortage of food. It is the Headman's responsibility to build up stocks. He has first to make his men throw off their natural sloth and go hunting, and he cannot tell them to do this in so many words. It is hard to picture a situation which you cannot resolve by the passing of a verbal message. The primitive societies depended, and some still depend, upon other means. The Headman has to create the hunting mood. He does that by means of his ritual of the hunting-dance. If it is to be buffalo, then the 'mood' of buffalo must inspire all their thoughts. He sets in motion his Buffalo Dance. Soon all the dancers are well on the way to become buffaloes. When the mood of the hunters has become sufficiently impregnated with buffalo, then the Headman switches his dance into the mood of killing, and by the rhythm and nature of his dance-gestures, whips his hunters into a frenzy to kill, and to kill buffalo. Once the tribe have reached a stage of possession which only buffalo-killing can satisfy, he turns them loose on the quarry, certain that the tribal larder will be filled before the mood is allowed to die away.

I have drawn this somewhat lurid picture of medicine-dancing in order to stress the point that dancing has, for countless ages, been a means to an end, the unifying bond of tribal society, and the most potent instrument of government in the hands of the tribal leader. All native dancing has something of this practical application. The fact that it can exercise such practical effect has tended to connect it with magical and superstitious beliefs of every conceivable kind. One widespread belief which clings to the practice of the primitive dance is that man, through the very simple act of jigging upon the surface of the ground, can communicate the vitality and exhilaration of the living to the recent dead, and through to the spirits of far-off ancestors, and ultimately to the underworld gods themselves.

The field of primitive religion is too esoteric to discuss in these pages in any detail. If, therefore, some of the generalisations that follow seem too sweeping, I hope that the reader will be indulgent and, before condemning the author, will seek further information in the works listed in the bibliography. The religious aspect of dancing is generally defined as a form of communication with the unseen forces which control tribal welfare and human survival, which provide food, promote fertility and regulate the weather. These forces are frequently conceived as representing the spirit of the race, either in the form of ancestral ghosts or as some still more nebulous deity that has to be coaxed or placated. One almost universal religious application of primitive dance is the transmission of vigour to the departed, so as to encourage them to strive for the common good of the living. Primitive man stamps upon the ground, and believes that his stamping rhythms reach those who have been buried. This naïve idea of the communication of energy may be found at the root of many tribal customs devoted to athletic prowess. The Olympic Games found their origin in such a primitive religious impulse.

As the faith behind such primitive religious impulses weakens, the dances which express it are not immediately abandoned, but they gradually change their character. The form of the ritual remains, but some of the mystery and magical content departs. The dancer becomes less and less of a medicine-maker and more and more a performing artist. In fact, the ritual changes imperceptibly into art. It was in some such manner that the folk-dances in the different parts of Europe grew out of old pagan rites as the pagans themselves were converted to Christianity and gradually lost their primitive beliefs. In those parts of Europe where the peasantry have remained relatively unchanged, and where Christianity has not made more than a surface impression, the local folk-dances still have a surprising amount of pagan belief and magic ritual adhering to them. Where the peasant culture has been wholly replaced by civilised Christendom, the ceremonial dances, that have managed to survive at all, tend to be somewhat pale reflections of the vital

4. Basque Characters from the Folk Play: Man–Woman,
Hobby Horse and Sweeper.

5. 'Snap', a Mediaeval Dragon from Norwich. This animal character was carried in processions of the Mayor and Corporation on Guild Days from 1451 until the passing of the Municipal Corporation Reform Act.

things they once were.   There are exceptions, however. In the most highly industrialised country in the world, England, there are still a few ancient rituals directly descended from the pre-Christian era, and retaining, to a surprising degree, their aura of primitive magic.

A completely different aspect of dancing which we in Europe have inherited from a less distant past has more to do with the use of our hands than of our feet.   If, in Norway, for instance, at a country gathering, you ask a local girl to dance, she puts one hand in yours and seeks with the other a neighbouring couple.   This instinct to link up together in a dance is implicit in the social dance gatherings of the whole of Northern Europe.   It comes to us by way of an old religious ritual, which, for many centuries, Christianity found no reason to discourage.   The primitive belief upon which this linking dance depends is also that of communication, but communication throughout the living community rather than with the souls of the departed. The oldest form of the linked dance is probably the endless chain, with a leader at the head to guide the company along a path of his own choosing.   While the element of linking and of sharing experience seems to predominate, there is plenty of evidence of other associated ideas.   In some primitive cultures, for instance, the actual path to be danced was an initiation into a new adult life, or it was a preparation and education for the journey from this world to the next. In that way, there is a direct connection between the chain dance, the maze, and the whole series of complicated tribal customs which reached their zenith in the construction of the Labyrinth in Crete.

The pre-Christian religious occasion in Northern

c

Europe, which was celebrated by chain dancing, was the arrival of Summer. It is still locally celebrated on the first of May and at Whitsuntide. The older type of chain dance, although extinct in England, is still performed in the Faroe Islands. The dance starts with a song sung by the leader, who decides his own steps and dances these as he sings. With his right hand he grasps the hand of any chance person who happens to be standing by. Other dancers link on haphazard, irrespective of age and of sex. All join in the singing and, following the step sequence set by the leader, the chain develops into a living community united in one purpose. This sung chain dance was once common in Mediæval Europe. It was particularly developed in England, so much so that it gave us our reputation for 'carolling'. We have forgotten this sense of 'carol', but words related to it still convey something of the community idea, such as 'chorus' and 'choric'. These link us with surviving chain dances in other parts of Europe, such as the 'Hora' and the 'Kolo' in the Balkans.

Having lost our word 'carol', we no longer have an epithet to identify this chain dance, and yet it is the source of the largest body of folk-dances which survived the passing of the Middle Ages. From the pagan Whitsuntide and May Day festivals have come the Maypole round dances, and the long processionals, which, because of their connection with country gatherings, became known as Country Dances. The habit of singing, while dancing, was never quite lost, but the use of instrumental music to accompany the dancers made further developments and new creations possible. The original 'carols' sank into oblivion. In the round dances and the processionals the unit of the dance became the couple—man and woman. One can only surmise that the haphazard assortment of persons now found in the Faroe Island chain dance, and probably the normal association in the earlier type of carol, was replaced by the regular alternation of man and woman. The formal dances of bower and hall that succeeded the mediæval carolling were all couple dances, the whole company forming a continuous procession round the hall, though each couple remained a separate unit. This distinction between the couple dance of the gentry and the linked dance of the country people was maintained until the dance of the country people eventually invaded the Court and was adopted by Society in Tudor times.

Another linked-up type of folk-dance appears from a different direction in a dramatic ritual performed in the middle of winter. This linked-up ritual is not a social community celebration in the sense that everyone joins in, but is a specialised rite, carried out by a select body of young men, chosen to carry out the responsibility and peculiar difficulties of the mid-winter rite. In this ritual the link may be a sword, a trade implement, a garland, a willow wand or a kerchief, and the significance lies not so much in the fact of linkage as in the drama expressed in the ritual. This 'Sword Dance', as we can conveniently describe it, requires separate consideration and is given a chapter all to itself. (See Chapter IV.)

* * * *

The primitive dancer engaged in communicating his vitality by leaps and stamps is himself brought under the spell of rhythm and loses his own self-conscious identity. He becomes, in fact, possessed, and ceases to be himself, and the ritual that enwraps him turns him into an actor. How much of the control exercised by the medicine-man upon his tribal dancers depends on his powers as a dancer, and how much of his ability as an actor, cannot be determined precisely. Dance and dramatic expression, when employed at a primitive level in religious ritual, are one and the same thing. We invent a special meaning which we attach to the words if we say that the quick, lively movements are dancing, while the slower gesticulations are drama. Both are elements of ritual. It is only when these primitive elements of expression are freed from the over-rule of religious ritual that they develop into their specific, separate arts. In the culture of ancient Greece the specific separation had not yet been made, and dance, drama and music were still integral parts of the ritual of religion. To a certain extent this unity of the various arts continued up to the time of the Renaissance, and it is this unifying force which pervades the great paintings and sculpture of that era.

Conversion to Christianity did not destroy, nor even wholly stifle, the older forms of religious drama. In fact, some of the old ritual was adopted by the early Church and embodied in its own practices. The yearly cycle of Miracle and Morality dramas, which played such an important part in the conversion to Christianity of the ignorant and illiterate peasantry in England, owed much of their appeal to the familiar pagan material which was wisely included in their presentation. But outside the control of the Church popular custom continued to practise one relic of the old religion in the form of a midwinter drama/dance

performance, in which was portrayed by the actor/
dancers a contest between life and death. The
European folk-dances performed during the winter
season, particularly between Michaelmas and Plough
Monday, all include some scraps of this old drama of
life and death. It has received much attention from
scholars of all kinds, and the literature dealing with it is
extensive, for it has served as part of the evidence in the
great study of comparative religion. What is invariably
portrayed in the folk-drama, acted on or near Christmas
Day, is a symbolic death and resurrection. This death
and revival drama, performed at the turn of the
year, is known in every European country. As one
would expect, it is found most complete among the
surviving peasantry, particularly among the primitive
peasantry in Eastern Europe. The play opens with
the self-sacrifice of an old man who, after identifying
himself with the sun, has a baby who grows up into the
replica of himself. This son, assisted by a number of
brothers, kills the old father. From his dead figure
arises, Phœnix-like, a young father who takes up the
torch and continues to guard and guide his community. In England, where one would hardly expect
to find much evidence of primitive and pagan custom,
the play, in fact, has been widespread and is performed in some localities at the present time. The type
of dance associated with it is described in Chapter IV.
We can distinguish between the Sword-Dance Play and
the Mummer's Play (without any Sword Dance). The
Sword-Dance Play usually opens with the Fool, acting
the part of an old man and clearing a space for the
action to come with a besom or a sword. He addresses
the audience and informs them of his own importance,

and then 'calls on' the other characters. At some point he is joined by a dancer impersonating a woman, and a love-scene takes place. During this love-scene the couple are interrupted by the Fool's eldest son, a rival for the affections of the 'woman'. The Fool then calls upon the other dancers to show themselves, and after introducing each severally to the spectators, they perform the first part of the Sword Dance. Each man holding the sword in his right hand, the dancers circle round, clashing their swords high above their heads. They then join up into a continuous ring, each man holding in his left hand the point of his neighbour's sword, and, linked in this way, they weave and plait a number of figures, culminating in the final figure, which is called the 'Lock' or the 'Knot'. In this figure the swords are interlaced to form a six- or eight-pointed star, according to the number of dancers. The 'Lock' is used both as a wheel to symbolise the sun and as a mechanism for the mock hanging or beheading of the Fool. There may be several unsuccessful rehearsals of the killing, and after each such passage the dance is resumed and another series of figures is performed, ending as before with the 'lock'. Finally the ritual death is successfully accomplished, and the scene is then set for the resurrection. In some plays the Fool revives himself, but in others a Doctor is introduced to bring the 'dead' man to life again. After the revival there is a celebration, in which audience and actors join together in a simple community dance.

Any interpretation of this folk-drama surviving in England would be very speculative were it not for the illumination given to it by examples found in other parts of Europe. They, in their turn, might be still somewhat obscure were it not possible to compare them with examples recorded still farther afield in other parts of the world and among very different peoples. For instance, the story would be incomplete if it did not include a reference to that remarkable cycle of religious dance-ritual performed in the Island of Malekula in Polynesia. Here the tribal drama had become so comprehensive and so complicated that its complete enactment occupied a period of thirty years, and the whole island community lived in a continual condition of acting a part. If the reader wishes to delve into that fascinating story, or is curious to know how our own drama sprang originally from a religious source, he must seek his own clue in the bibliography. Once he sets out in a particular direction he will not find it easy to stop. Here we must look to our own ancient seasonal customs to provide our chief clues. So let us turn back to European customs, with which more people are familiar and to which our English dances are closely related. We dance them to-day because we find them vital, beautiful forms and not because they once possessed some magical significance. If I discuss old customs, it is for the light they throw on the history and origin of our dances and not because I think the customs themselves have now any validity.

III

The Morisco

AMONG the old European seasonal customs preserved
by the peasantry, two stand out as holding obvious
significance for those who practise them, in spite of
conversion to Christianity more than a thousand years
ago. These two customs fall, one within the period
between Michaelmas and Shrove Tuesday, and the
other between Shrove Tuesday and Palm Sunday.
The first, the mid-winter custom, is rich in the
Sword Dance survivals discussed in the next chapter.
The second period, which roughly corresponds to
Christian Lent, is characterised by an athletic dance
performed by a cast of young men chosen for their
vigour and vitality. This young men's dance can still
be seen in many parts of Europe, including the Pyrenees,
Italy, Austria and all the countries of the Balkan
Peninsula. There is reason to think that it was not the
monopoly of any one country, but that it was once
embedded in the early culture of the whole of Northern
Europe. Anthropologists who have compared the
young men's dance of Europe with the dances of native,
savage tribes, interpret it as a kind of dynamo, furnishing
an output of energy with which to quicken all growing
things and ensure future fertility and the food supply.
Some authorities argue that the stream of energy produced by the dancers was by them conceived to quicken

the dead and to enable them, as messengers, to hasten
their passage through the underworld to reach the
gods or the spirits of their ancient ancestors who had
gone long before. With the aid of those spirits of the
underworld, the living above ground were able to
influence destiny and to improve the prospects of the
community. However we interpret the ritual the
expression of living vitality is patent.

The young men leap and stamp—their rhythmical
actions are emphasised by the sound of bells and by the
fluttering ribbons. The whole effect, even to the most
sceptic observer, is one of tremendous vitality. This
old pagan ritual has been preserved, so far as Europe
is concerned, most comprehensively among the peasants
of Rumania. The Calusari, or 'fairies', (literally
'Little Horses') are a select body of men, in fact, a
secret society, and the team picked to perform the
annual ritual are vowed to devote themselves to a daily
ceremony for a period of over forty days, starting on
Shrove Tuesday and carrying on until Palm Sunday.
They are dressed in a most festive and highly coloured
costume, garnished with ribbons, shining pieces of
metal and bells. Accompanying these beautiful figures
are one or more contrasting ugly characters, the
animal-men. The team normally has a couple of
fiddlers who provide their music. They carry with
them a short Maypole, on the top of which is fastened
a small bunch of freshly-gathered garlic. Starting in
the early morning, the whole team go through an
initiation rite—each man, including the musicians,
being beaten with the stout staves carried by each
dancer, on his body and on the soles of his feet. The
animal-men, who are hard to catch, are given specially

rough treatment. The normal form of the dance is an open-ring formation with a series of highly elaborate stamping steps and a long stride-walk which carries the group from place to place. The animal-man behaves as a rough clown—sometimes frightening the spectators and sometimes amusing them. The next stage of the ritual presents a play, acted inside the ring of 'Fairy' dancers, made by each man holding his stave and that of the man next to him to form a linked-up circle. Inside this 'house', with the animal-men occasionally jumping in and out like freaks of nature without a 'by your leave', a wooing and marriage ceremony takes place. The home is then invaded by an interloper and a fight ensues. This drama ends with a death and resurrection, and the dancers move their living stage to some other spot and continue to dispense more of their magic medicine to the community. Late in the day the young mothers bring out their sick babies. Each of the 'Fairies' gives his dance 'treatment' to a sick child. He jigs about with a baby in his arms, then he lays the infant down on the ground and capers and hops round and over it. At length he hands the baby back to the mother, who goes away satisfied that the medicine will be effective. The final scene shows the young medicine-men in their open ring with the whole community pressing in around them. Especially eager are the unmarried girls, seeking to rub shoulders with one of the dancing Fairies. In the Kolo, or chain dance, which follows, and in which all the community join, the magic of vitality and fertility is broadcast to those dancing. The young girls who have succeeded in touching one of the Fairies know that they will soon find a husband and rear a happy family.

In other parts of Europe only broken fragments of this elaborate ritual have been preserved. The dramatic fragment, with its plot of death and resurrection, and of a contest between the forces of life and death, is to be found in many countries. The dispensing of medicine and fertility by the dancers is not quite so widespread. No doubt this was much more discouraged by the Church, but the young men who dance, flutter ribbons, ring bells and blacken their faces have survived in many places. In England this dance was, until recent times, a commonplace throughout the Cotswolds. It was performed in many towns in Lancashire and Cheshire, and appears frequently in literary and historical references. It was as familiar to Shakespeare and as much a part of his native environment as the swans on the Avon. He called the dance the 'Morisco', and it is this name that appears so often in literature, but its more popular title is simply the Morris Dance. Why the 'Young Men's Dance' should be called 'Morris' in England is a story that has taken quite a long time to sort out. The explanation normally given, that the dance came from Morocco, is mere nonsense. Morris or Morisco, meaning 'Moorish', need not imply anything more significant than that the dancers had blackened faces. It is part and parcel of ritual folk ceremonies for the dancers to disguise themselves with masks or paint. The blackened face has always been the most complete disguise easily available to everyone. The appearance of the young men disguised as blackamoors is enough in itself to attach the name 'Moorish' to the 'Young Men's Dance'. A further possible explanation is that, on both sides of the Pyrenees, where this same 'Young

Men's Dance' persists as a living tradition, the seasonal festivals include one called the 'Mauresque', in which is staged a contest between the Moors and Christians, in itself a dramatic representation of the annual conflict between life and death, older than Christendom. The Mauresque must have often been seen by our English army of occupation in Gascony and Aquitaine during the Hundred Years' War. Soldiers returning on furlough fresh from contact with the local Basque dance festivals would compare these with their own English dances. Their similarity to the Mauresque would prompt them to attach to the English dance a name so descriptive of the black face, and so suited to the antics of the local dancers. It seems certain that the name was imported, but it is equally certain that the dance itself was not—at least, not at the same time. A still simpler explanation is that the word 'Moorish' was used in the sense of 'pagan', and the Morris was a pagan dance. This 'Young Men's Dance', dedicated to the forty days of Pagan Lent, was probably indigenous to these Islands as far back as Roman times. It must have been brought by some of the earliest of our invading ancestors. Its geographical distribution in England relates it to the oldest settlements in England. In the Cotswolds the Morris Dance maintained its grip upon country life until about a hundred years ago. Then village life, indirectly affected by the industrial revolution, began rapidly to change, and the communities to decay. The building of the Great Western Railway, for instance, drew young men away to new concentrations of humanity, to places like Swindon. Many of the teams of Morris dancers died out at this time. The few that survived this big change continued on to the end of the

19th century, but there was, for once in a thousand years, no new generation of young men dancers to fill the depleted ranks. Universal education and the new 'town' attitude of slight contempt towards old-established country ways were enough to blight the old country customs. When Cecil Sharp met the Headington Morris team in 1899, he saw the rear-guard of what had been once a great company. There is one other village that has maintained its Morris up to the present day, entirely owing to the obstinacy and tenacity of the leader and musician. William Wells of Bampton-in-the-Bush, eighty years of age and blind these last ten years, is a living representative of our extinct peasantry, a real countryman and one of nature's gentlemen. Although he has not seen his team perform for a long time, and it is easy to criticise his dancers' performance, yet he and they together are still dispensing the old medicine. To come round a corner on Whit Monday, the Bampton Festival day, and to see the dancers in their white clothes, tinkling bells and fluttering ribbons, picked out against a Cotswold stone wall, is an experience that one cannot forget. Sharp noted down the dances at Headington and at Bampton from complete team performances. In other Cotswold villages he had to be content with survivors of teams otherwise defunct. In Ilmington, for instance, Sharp had to get his information from individual dancers and not from a complete team. The sole surviving traditional dancer, Sam Bennett, singer and fiddler as well as Morris dancer, has devoted practically the whole of his life to the preservation of his local songs, tunes and dances. He remembers the words of most of the dance-tunes and is insistent on the

importance of the stock characters, including the
Hobby Horse, of which he has, in his possession, a very
fine example.

The names of the Oxfordshire, Northamptonshire and
Gloucestershire villages have become familiar to the
thousands of dancers who have tried to master the dance
movements of the village traditions. Longborough
and Bledington, Sherborne and Field Town, Bucknell
and Brackley, Eynsham and Abingdon are the names of
picturesque Cotswold villages, but they are also the
names of different types of Morris Dance—each type
or tradition with a character and style all its own.

The name 'Morris' was not restricted to the Cotswold dances. England has other dances that resemble
the Mauresque of France and Spain. There are men's
dances in Lancashire, Cheshire and Derbyshire familiar
to the local people and accepted as casually as the local
scenery. The Lancashire Morris seems always to have
been associated with the rush-bearing season, when the
new floors were laid in barn and hall to keep man and
beast warm through the winter. The fact that the
Northern Morris Dance was held at a different time of
the year from the Cotswold dance does not worry the
folk-lorist. The changes made in the calendar, and
the difficulty of fixing the old feasts on to the new style
of counting dates, are quite enough to explain how
spring customs could be shifted to the summer or
autumn.

The best known of the surviving Lancashire Morris
teams is that of Royton, near Oldham. This dance is
performed by a team of ten men—four aside, with
'centres' at each end—led by a 'Squire' or 'Manager',
who calls the figures and occasionally blows a whistle,

like a football referee. The dance is performed to the
music of a concertina and drum band. Much of its
character is given by the 'slings' which take the place
of the Cotswold Morris handkerchief. These slings
are made of a length of raw cotton fibre, stitched into a
cotton bag and forming a thin sausage about 1 foot
long and ½ inch in diameter. While the dancers are
performing their clog-dance steps the slings are twirled
round by a quick action of the wrist, giving an extra-
ordinary sense of vigour and vitality. On their leather
clogs the men wear little bells, fastened into the shoe-
laces. They dance in black-velvet breeches, trimmed
with white lace, a white shirt covered with crossed
sashes, and held together by a broad cummerbund.
Round the neck are worn three strings of beads, the
lower one reaching to waist level, and the whole series
carefully held in place by a number of safety-pins.
Crowning each dancers' head is a neat little jockey cap,
with a sharp peak.

An astonishing example of the Lancashire Morris
still performed in Bacup, is danced by eight dancers who
are completely black from head to foot, except for a
white or coloured hat, short white skirt, and white
stockings. It receives its particular character from the
dance properties which are worn by the dancers on the
palms of their hands and on their waists and knees.
These properties are little wooden discs, called 'nuts',
the size of castanets but composed only of single discs.
These are clapped in time to the music with a curious
rolling gesture: the hand disc tapping first the waist
disc, then reaching down to the knee disc and up again
to the waist, making a continuous clatter quite barbaric
in its nature. The figures, a mixture of chains and

circles, are very similar to those of the Calusari of Rumania, and the whole effect is one of magic and mystery.

The name 'Morris' is, in some parts of England, applied to the actors or Mummers who act the 'Folk Play' of the mid-winter festival depicting death and resurrection. It is no wonder that there has been some confusion over the name 'Morris' Dance, when it is a label tied to so many different folk customs. Cecil Sharp usually narrowed the application of the name to the Cotswold dance on which he himself lavished so much time and attention. To-day most people who know the dance at all would interpret the name within those narrow limits. The other types of Morris are called the Lancashire Morris or Derbyshire Morris to distinguish them from the Cotswold or Oxfordshire dances.

As in the case of the Country Dance, there must have been a good deal of interchange between the dancers from the country places with the townspeople who copied country custom. In the Masques, organised by the nobility and squires in their country houses, the local dancers were frequently invited to take part in an episode. The gentry would not hesitate to incorporate some of the Morris steps into their own dances, and the Morris dancers would, of course, see strange and new-fangled capers which they themselves would adopt if they thought fit. One printed description of an Elizabethan Masque refers to a performance by the local Morris dancers, and also to a performance by the travelled gentry, of a replica of one of the contests between Christians and Moors they had seen during a journey into Italy. With the ancient living tradition

6. A Cotswold Morris Dance.

7. The Bacup Coco-nut Dancers.   The 'nuts' are seen strapped to hands, w
and knees.

of the Morris of the country people, appearing side by side with the related but imported Morisco, it is no wonder that there has been confusion over the meaning of the Morris Dance. One thing I consider now proven is that the story of the importation of the dance itself from France or Northern Spain by John of Gaunt, or his officers, is false. They may have brought the name, but the dance to which they applied it had been an ancient English custom long before their day.

Another example of a Lancashire Morris Dance which has preserved old elements of some interest is the Abram Circle Dance. Abram is situated a few miles from Wigan. The ceremony, recently discontinued, was held in June. The dance used to go on for two or three days on a special piece of ground (called 'the Morris dancers' ground'), set aside and kept for their use, and so long as one performance at least was given there every twenty-one years, it could not be used for anything else. The dance itself is very simple in character: pairs of dancers revolve round a centre like a merry-go-round. The final figure brings the dancers to the centre to make salutation to the central characters—a King and Queen, who carried between them a garland. The garland was a wooden erection, shaped like a bee-hive, borne on top of a pole about 6 feet in length, made of wooden hoops, and trimmed with leaves and ribbons. Silver watches and other silver ornaments were suspended from it and a silver teapot was placed on top. This is the description given by Miss Karpeles in her monograph, published in the *Journal of the E.F.D.S.* in 1932. The garland was locally called 'the Bush'. Mirrors and ribbons are universally associated with the men's Spring Dance,

D

representing sunshine and vitality. The green bush is itself the token of the re-awakened life, symbolised throughout the North Temperate Zone by green shoots, springing buds and fruit-blossoms of every kind. It is therefore, to be expected that vegetation should be found associated with a dance which celebrates growth, and renewed vigour. The Rumanian 'Fairies' carry with them their Maypole, the top garnished with a sprig of flowering garlic, and a white handkerchief, the symbol of lightness as opposed to sadness or heaviness.

The 'Bush' had many strange applications. As a Bower it functioned as a mobile hostelry during the spring celebrations. Erected in the Morris villages at some convenient place near a crossroads, a popular location for the Morris dancers, the Ale Bower was constructed so that a man inside had room to prepare and serve drinks to the thirsty dancers and the cheerful bystanders. The practice of building such springtime bowers has died out in this country.

Men who served behind the Bower, or Bar, were often called 'Mr. Green', or 'Jack Green', but the name of 'Jack-in-the-Green' has been more specifically applied to a mobile bush which paraded with the dancers and took part in the dance performances. This Jack-in-the-Green was a familiar figure in many parts of England, particularly in London, until recent times. Formerly associated with groups of Morris dancers, and the other dramatis personæ of the 'Folk Play', it became an independent figure, and, under the special patronage of the chimney-sweeps, who have always been associated with the springtime festival, Jack-in-the-Green might have been seen on any holiday occasion up to the beginning of this century. Charles

Dickens in 'Sketches by Boz' devotes a chapter to May Day in London which includes a vivid description of the Jack-in-the-Green and his attendant sweeps. But the merry spirit of May had evidently begun to droop even in his day.

Representation of a vegetation sprite or a Jack-in-the-Green can be traced back in history to our oldest permanent monuments, cathedrals and churches, where he is a recurring figure in the decoration and design of stone-carving and tracery, and in the carvings of choir-stalls. Peeping through a delicate screen of twigs and leaves may be distinguished a nose and a mouth and two eyes, and, sometimes, a pair of ears which stick out beyond the edges of the screen. A more common form is to show the face with sprays of greenery growing out of the ears and mouth. Lady Raglan made a study of the Green Man in church decoration, and a list of examples is given in her monograph, published in *Folk-Lore*, the Journal of the Folk-Lore Society, in 1939.

The particular Green Man who has a proprietory interest in the Morris Dance is that semi-mythical character, Robin Hood, the hero of so many stories and ballads, and the patron of our ancient English cult of the long bow. Robin-of-the-Wood is another name for Jack-in-the-Green, and long before the reigns of King Richard and King John he was a local medicine-man— a character in the ritual drama concerned with the restoration of life after the winter death. The Robin Hood Games, which included such characters known as Maid Marian, Friar Tuck, Hobby Horse and Little John, were romanticised versions of the ritual Folk Play. Robin Hood, the central figure, had to die and

come to life again like the ritual actor, and his Maid
Marian was that common symbol of fertility, the man-
woman. If the fertility aspect of Robin Hood and
Maid Marian kept the game popular with the English
peasantry, it was his symbolic death which maintained
him in the myth preserved by tradition and literature.
He was killed by the chance flight of an arrow and bled
to death. Comparative folk-lore has shown that other
local gods, who were constrained to give their lives for
their people, have suffered death from a shaft. The
association of this ancient myth of Robin-of-the-Wood
with the leader of a band of rob-the-rich-help-the-poor
outlaws in Sherwood Forest, and with the national
need for a high level of skill with the long bow, has
provided us with enough literary and dramatic substance to serve popular taste for romance, mixed with
magic, for the last seven hundred years.

The stained-glass window formerly at Betley Priory,
Staffordshire, and now preserved at Minsterley, Shrop-
shire, shows a group of Morris dancers accompanied by
a Hobby Horse, a Maid Marian and a Friar Tuck.
This picture shows the stock dramatic characters from
the Folk Play attendant on the dancers in the particular
guise of a particular period. At the beginning of the
19th century the stock characters were not Robin Hood,
but such heroes as Nelson, Wellington or Napoleon.
In our time, had the custom maintained itself, the
characters would have appeared as Alexander, Mont-
gomery or Mountbatten.

It is impossible to relate the story of the Green Man
in all his aspects, but two further instances may be
given, for they serve as connections with other customs,
with their attendant dances. One is the story of John

Barleycorn, who, as the figure or corn baby made out of the last sheaf of corn cut in the field, is the acknowledged corn spirit. He comes to life through the ploughed sods, grows to full stature and acquires a beard, to be cut down in his prime. After providing the food and drink essential to life, he returns to the soil to start the life-cycle all over again. This corn figure, plaited from the last sheaf, or 'nek', was not only acclaimed by all the harvesters, but hung up in the church until its place could be taken by the new figure made from the 'nek' of the following year.

The other story is of Jack Straw, once the central figure in a London procession. Attended by Morris dancers, chimney-sweeps, Jacks-in-the-Green, Hobby Horses, Dragons and Maid Marians, Jack Straw was borne in a cart up to Hampstead Heath on Shrove Tuesday. He stayed there for forty days as a cock-shy for everyone, and then on Palm Sunday he was ceremonially burned. His ashes were carefully collected and sold in little twists of paper, each a talisman and a symbol of good luck.

When the Morris Dance of the Cotswolds was described by Cecil Sharp, he and other experts put forward theories in an endeavour to account for them. One view was that the Morris Dance had been derived from the Sword Dance by the simple process of substituting first of all a stick for the sword, and later, substituting a handkerchief for the stick. This view gains some measure of support from the fact that many of the Central European linked dances are danced with sticks and with withies, and there are, of course, many examples of such chain dances as the Farandole and Cramignon, where the kerchief is used as a link between some of the dancers taking part. The linked handkerchief dance occurs in a number of Cotswold village traditions, and so the suggestion does not seem unreasonable. A study of the geographical distribution, however, shows that the dance types are so grouped as to suggest that the Cotswold Morris was established in England before the Sword Dance. It is, in fact, now generally accepted that the practice of the Sword Dance and the Folk Play that goes with it was probably introduced by the Danes about one thousand years ago. The Cotswold Morris, on the other hand, must have been indigenous in the Midlands of England ages before this. In fact, so far back that we can only fumble at the date. These two different types of dance seem to belong to the cultures of two different peoples who settled in England at widely separated times. If the dances have something in common, we must seek the common origin further back in antiquity, when these two peoples shared a common culture.

If we simply regard the Cotswold Morris Dance as an example of that Young Men's Dance evolved for the purpose of quickening Nature in the spring, that is sufficient explanation of its character. The group of men are initiated specialists; the form of dance is a procession, circle or square to frame the attendant characters, the movements and the bells are merely the paraphernalia of rhythm, while the white handkerchiefs, white clothes and the ribbons and feathers with which they are decorated, represent that immaterial or spiritual side of man and nature shared by the living and the dead. The Lancashire Morris Dances, although the dancers use different properties, are clearly related to the Cotswold Morris Dances. The

Derbyshire Morris Dances, on the other hand, do introduce an added element to the idea of the procession. The two files of dancers are organised as two distinct 'sides' which are differently dressed. One side (the man's side), is dressed in plain white clothes and untrimmed white hats, whereas the clothes of the other side are garnished with coloured scarves and their hats are gaily decorated. The two sides, when they move in procession, are opposite one another, and the stationary dances which they perform are possibly the relics of the life and death contest, an element which has apparently been lost in the Cotswold and Lancashire Morris Dances.

*　　　　*　　　　*　　　　*

At the time of Cecil Sharp's death in 1924, many of his friends and fellow-workers thought that most of the Morris Dance material which he set out to find had been located. Sharp had worked thoroughly and systematically, and he never failed to follow up a clue. How completely his work had been done was subsequently borne out by the contributions that came from other sources and the various pieces of research that have been undertaken by other collectors and scholars during the last twenty years. As already stated, a considerable number of local traditional country dances have been recorded. A few more Morris Dances and Sword Dances have been noted. Apart from these, there has been little fresh material. Nearly all the folk tunes and songs since recorded are variants of the Sharp versions. But some of his original sources have outlived the collector, and have served to guide the E.F.D.S. in its work of dissemination.

William Kimber, literally the father of the folk-dance revival in England, has never ceased to exercise a parental eye upon the movement which he helped to start. He has often been critical of the Society's teaching, and it has been fortunate to have been able to refer points of doubt and difficulty to such a reliable upholder of tradition.

Much has been learned of the practice of Morris dancing during the years since Sharp's death. Sharp himself had no previous dance experience when he embarked on his task of recording and teaching, and he was remarkably successful in inventing a form of dance notation which can be readily interpreted. But it was only towards the end of his lifetime that he was in a position to estimate the full significance of the material upon which he had been engaged. With the subsequent visits of dancers from other countries in Europe, the English dancers' appreciation and understanding of their own traditions widened and deepened. Our picture of the English Morris as a man's ritual, linked with the pre-Christian Lenten festival, would be blurred and fragmentary if it reflected only the English survivals. Gradually the picture has been filled in by examples from other lands and, with a vision widened by such examples, the English dancers continue to discover fresh aspects of their own familiar dance forms.

The Bampton traditional Morris, the repertory of which was recorded by Cecil Sharp in the early part of the century, has continued without a break to dance each year. Their performance may be witnessed on any Whit Monday. Sharp's original description of the dances does not fit exactly the present method of performance by the Bampton team. The difference is due to the small changes continually taking place in the performances of all traditional dancers. Such process of change is an essential element in the traditional character of folk-dance and folk-music. But the difference noticeable in performance by the Bampton dancers of to-day may, in some part, be ascribed to the inherent difficulty of noting down any Morris Dance and of interpreting the written notation. My own experience as a dancer of the Morris has been continuous for thirty-five years, yet more than ever do I realise the practical difficulty of extracting what is significant in a dance movement. In the Morris Dance, arms and legs work together in close co-ordination. One notices that these co-ordinated movements of the limbs grow out of pulsations of the whole body as ultimate expressions of those pulsations. The fact that Morris Dance movements are natural and spontaneous makes this matter of observation even more difficult. I suggest to the reader that he makes his own attempt to write down, in some form of notation, the relative movements made by his two arms and two legs in the act of walking, and he will at once appreciate the nature of the problem. To solve this difficulty Sharp depended more on his own personal teaching, and that of his immediate assistants, than on his published works. Even so, there has been a tendency, apparently inevitable, to diverge from the original movements and to produce, among all those who came to learn, a style of action and co-ordination of movements which failed to capture the rhythm and the traditional manner. The only solution to this problem of gradual departure from dance tradition has been to have periodic refreshment at the traditional source.

In the case of those dances where local tradition has kept them alive, the Society has endeavoured to follow this policy since Cecil Sharp's death.

Some of the earliest efforts to keep in touch with the traditional Morris were made by groups of undergraduates from the Universities, particularly of Cambridge, who instituted the practice of a 'Travelling Morrice' team which visited and re-visited the Cotswold villages where Sharp had collected his material in the decades before. It was not an infrequent occurrence on these tours for an old man to appear in the village street, and, after applauding the dancing of the undergraduates, to announce himself as one of the old local Morris 'Side' and to criticise the performance that had just been given, illustrating his points with gestures and steps. These visits of young dancers to the old haunts went on throughout the years between the wars, and the information obtained as a result of them has done much to extend our knowledge of the Morris Dance.

The growing influence of the revival also had its effect on some of the local dances that had lapsed. Survivors of teams, noting the growing public interest in the various types of folk-dance, were prompted to revive their own local customs. Two of the Cotswold Morris villages, encouraged by the prospect of taking part in one of the national festivals, not only produced a representative team for the occasion, but managed to restore the annual custom, which then continued up to the outbreak of the recent war. From time to time during the last century local customs which lapsed temporarily were revived by the conscious stimulus of a local enthusiast. The annual festivals in London provided an even stronger incentive that appealed to all parts of the country. During the fifteen years prior to 1939, when groups of foreign dancers and traditional English teams met at the annual performance at the Albert Hall in London, the public appreciation of the different types of folk-dance grew steadily. Two examples of the Lancashire Morris Dance were seen in London for the first time during that period, and some of the ritual customs mentioned later in this book were brought to these Festivals. The English dancers learned much from each other, but they learned even more from their continental friends of the basic technique of folk-dancing. This aspect of international exchange of folk-dance experience is one that appeals powerfully to all dancers.

Fortified by this refreshment, the Society is now far better equipped for its task of restoring to the English their dances and their music. When we reflect on the moribund condition of the English folk tradition at the time when Cecil Sharp first began his work of investigation and revival, its present vitality is quite astonishing. Men's Morris Clubs meet and dance in many parts of England. They congregate together at regular intervals to share experience and skill. An International Council has been established to foster the study and encouragement of folk-music and dance throughout the world, and in every country some form of organisation now exists to promote its native art of dance and song.

IV

Dancing With Swords

AMONG the seasonal customs that fall between Michaelmas and Ash Wednesday, are the feast of Halloween,
of Old Christmas, the Twelve Days of Christmas and
Plough Monday. There are many surviving elements
of the old Christmas customs that deserve attention.
If I select the dramatic elements, I do so because of
their direct relation to the mid-winter folk-dance. So
much drama is implicit in this mid-winter dancing that
it would be more accurate to dub these dancers
'actors'. In the Young Men's Dance of Lent the action
of leaping and jigging was the prime factor in the
performance. In this mid-winter festival this type of
dance action is comparatively subordinate. The
actors that appear in the Christmas-tide drama include
not only the Fool, Man-Woman and Hobby Horse,
the stock characters already identified, but the players
of minor parts that have tagged on through the
centuries—some from casual contact with the legiti-
mate theatre and some possibly derived from characters
in the miracle plays. Ignoring these subsidiary
characters and cutting the story to the bone, there
emerge the central figure of the Fool or Medicine-
man, and his group of assistants who, disguised with
black faces, form a secret society, of which he himself
is the head. His 'act' is to suffer death in order that

the community shall survive. His 'sons' (the members of the secret society) have to kill the head of the house, their 'father'. While he acts this sacrifice he visits the underworld, taking with him all the accumulated evils, burdens and difficulties of the past year. When his task is done he returns, a revived leader, to resume his earthly responsibilities, fortified for a new year. This dramatic killing of a 'father' to be subsequently reborn for the good of the tribe is the germ of many religions. In its pagan form it survives in peasant custom in different parts of Europe. As a village diversion it has been noted and described in the British Isles from Land's End to John o' Groats. In England the 'Folk Play', as I shall now call it, has been found in its most ancient and uncorrupted form in the village of Revesby in Lincolnshire, preserved in a manuscript written at the end of the 18th century and deposited in the records of the church. (The text is printed in 'The Folk Play' of E. K. Chambers.) In this Folk Play the six sword dancers are introduced as the sons of the Fool, who plays the chief part. He proclaims to the assembly that his sons have come there to kill him: that he does not want to die just yet: but if he has to die that he will die for the good of everybody. The sons then performed a figure of a Sword Dance, which, although not described in detail, was no doubt a linked-up dance, the dancers holding the swords in their hands and making a continuous ring of steel. At the end of the figure they tie the 'Knot', or 'Lock', or 'Glass', consisting of a star made by meshing the swords into a close, compact mat which holds itself together. The Fool takes this 'Lock' and, after describing it as a fine large looking-glass in which he can see himself, he breaks it and stamps upon the pieces, telling his sons that he is not quite ready yet. They then perform another figure of the Sword Dance, which again ends in making the 'Glass'. This lock they place over his head, which they threaten to cut off. The Fool then plays for time by making his Will, leaving to each son a portion of property. Eventually he submits to the inevitable: they place their hands upon the hilts of the swords forming the 'necklace', withdraw their swords, and he falls 'dead'. But only for a moment. Before the actors can move from the spot, he jumps up and says that he still has another life. They start all over again. Once more they dance the figure, once more they tie the 'Lock', and once more he thinks of some dregs of property to leave them and so delay his fate. But at the last 'necklace' they appear to kill him. For a time he lies quite still and the 'sons' lament for the father they have cut down. They compare him to the evening sun, and question what is to become of them all. The Fool then comes to life and recounts how he has returned from a journey: that while he has been out of the world he has heard so much music, of fiddles playing and bells ringing, that he now has a mind to go away singing. A love scene follows in which the Fool and his eldest son vie with each other for possession of the Lady (a Man-Woman). The Fool wins the Lady, and the performance closes with all the actors joining in a final dance.

The student of Greek history will be struck by the close similarity with a ritual acted at the Feast of Dionysus, in which the Titans killed their 'father' while he was looking at himself reflected in a glass. One small difference between the Titans and the Revesby

actors is that while the latter disguised themselves by
blacking their faces with soot, the Titans did so by
whitening theirs with lime. The English Sword
Dance, which formed an integral part of the Folk Play
and provided the mechanism for the mock death, has
been found only in certain parts of the country, and
then mostly with the dramatic elements reduced to
mere fragments and the stock characters to irrelevant
shadows, fooling about on the outskirts of the dance
proper. It is confined to Yorkshire, Northumberland
and Durham.

In Yorkshire there are roughly half-a-dozen traditional teams who have kept up the ancient custom and
who still meet to dance at least once a year. The
practice must, at one time, have been quite widespread throughout Yorkshire, for the dance has been
found in places as far apart as Sheffield and Saltburn.
In the villages near Sheffield, round York, near Whitby
and in the Cleveland ironstone district, where the
dance survives, the inhabitants accept it as a custom
they have always known. In Goathland, the sense
of the custom as a seasonal festival is still very strong,
and the annual outing of the Plough Stots on Plough
Monday is the proper Sword Dance fixture of the year,
even if they do the dance at other times as a concession
to local entertainment. It may be of interest to compare two Sword Dance traditions, located near
Sheffield, and within a few miles of one another, which
have for generations maintained their distinctive
character.

In Grenoside, one of the two villages, the dance is
performed by six men wearing clogs and carrying
straight swords. Associated with it is a certain

amount of dialogue and a song, 'calling on' the dancers, sung by the leader, who brandishes a curved sabre and wears a cap of rabbit's skin, with the head of the animal set in front. The dancers tie the 'Lock' at the beginning of their performance, the leader (or 'Captain', as he is called) kneels down in the centre, and after the 'Lock' has been placed round his neck, the swords are drawn. His cap of skin is knocked off in the process and rolls on the ground, looking horribly like a decapitated head. The 'Captain' himself does not fall down to become the centre of a dramatic resurrection, but just slips away from the dance, which then continues on its course. At the very end of the Sword Dance is a special section known as 'Jolly Lads', which obviously celebrates the close of a successful ceremony.

In the neighbouring village of Handsworth the dance is for eight men, wearing boots and garters, and the style of dancing is different. There is no calling-on song, and only one action of dramatic significance. The 'Lock' is made at the end of the dance and hung over the leading dancer's neck, but no attempt is made to use it for dramatic purposes. The only trace of ritual ceremony that remains is in the opening figure, to which I will refer later, and in the dress, particularly in the head-gear worn by each dancer. This is a tight-fitting cap, decorated with two tufts of lamb's wool, one of which is dyed blood-red.

The North Skelton and Lingdale Sword Dances in Cleveland are interesting examples of a spontaneous local revival that took place nearly thirty years ago. The regular practice of the dance at the neighbouring village of Loftus had died out some time before the 1914 war, and Cecil Sharp had never encountered any of the

8. Bampton-in-the-Bush. Standing in front of the Morris side are the fiddler, William Wells, the Cake-Bearer, and the Fool.

9. The Marshfield Paper Boys, acting the Mummers' Play in the street.

surviving dancers, although he had been following Sword Dance clues in the North Riding since his first Sword Dance find at Kirkby Malzeard in 1906. Two survivors of the traditional Loftus team, named Winspear and Featherstone, living only some dozen miles apart, both had the idea of reviving their dance and teaching a new generation of men how to dance it. The circumstances which spurred them to this action were the revival of interest in folk-dancing, and the depression in the ironstone industry immediately after the 1914–1918 war, when the miners were forced to look round for other means to earn a livelihood. Winspear and Featherstone, both capable concertina and melodeon players, each started a team, and these teams went dancing in the streets and taking collections for their own benefit. Winspear's team was centred at North Skelton, and Featherstone's at Lingdale. When the local industry recovered, the teams still continued to perform regularly, becoming well known to folk-dance audiences in other parts of England as well as in their native Yorkshire. The skill of their dancing, cultivated in the street performances during the depression of 1919–1920, has since been something to marvel at.

When Winspear moved away from North Skelton, his place as musician was taken by George Tremain, who speedily made a name for himself, not only for his playing for sword dancing, but also as a folk-dance player at social gatherings and parties of all kinds. The tenacity of the Sword-Dance tradition has been demonstrated again in recent years. Despite the disruption of local life and country custom during the six years of the recent war, somehow the sword dancers

E

have managed to get their teams together again. The two teams in the Sheffield district, and those up in the Skelton region, as well as the boys' team of fishermen at Flamborough Head, have all performed since the end of the war. No doubt these local revivals, or rather survivals, owe much to Cecil Sharp's original pioneering. It was not until he had awakened interest in these local traditions and had given the dancers a new pride in their ancient custom, that the English as a whole began to realise what they possessed in the way of dance tradition. Wherever a performance of the English Sword Dance is witnessed it arouses enthusiasm and curiosity. On the thousands of dancers who have learned its intricacies it exercises a forcible appeal. Knowing its finer points, they relish the performance of any skilful team, and this large body of dancers have all contributed toward the encouragement of this traditional custom.

Cecil Sharp was able to recapture several sword dances, the practice of which had actually ceased, by tapping the memory of a retired performer, who, unlike Winspear or Featherstone, had not attempted to initiate a new team. The feats of memory of some of these ex-dancers are well-nigh incredible. Perhaps the most spectacular instance was the recovery of the Ampleforth Play and Sword Dance, which Cecil Sharp describes in full in the third volume of his 'Sword Dances of the North of England', originally published in 1913. His source of information was an ex-railwayman, then seventy-five years of age, named George Wright, who used on occasion to play the part of the Clown, or Fool, besides dancing the Sword Dance. The dramatic context is very complete, and, after the Revesby Play, forms the most interesting example of the Folk Play found in England. The dance is the most developed of all the Yorkshire Sword Dances, and it is fortunate that Mr. Wright was able to supply Sharp not only with the complete dialogue, including all the subsidiary parts and the songs, but the very complicated figures of the dance itself.

The village of Revesby, where that other version of the Folk Play was found, represents the most southern point in the geographical distribution of this type of dance in England. North of Yorkshire the dance is found right up through Northumberland (but danced with a different type of implement), almost to the Scottish Border. It is not found farther West, but is confined conspicuously to the area of the Danish place-names and of Danish settlement of about the 10th century. Dr. Needham's map showing the distribution of men's traditional dances (see p. 72) brings this point out very clearly. To find another example of the linked-up type of Sword Dance, one has to go North, passing over from Scotland to the Shetlands, to the Island of Papa Stour, where the linked Sword Dance and Folk Play are still performed. The Papa Stour play and dance are described by Sir Walter Scott in his novel 'The Pirate'. This play is based upon the story of the Seven Champions of Christendom, and the dialogue bears many points of resemblance to the Revesby Play. It is now clear that both dance and ritual actions are older even than the patron saints used in this case as labels for the stock characters. The distribution of this Sword Dance indicates that England received it from the Germanic peoples, and probably mainly from the Danes. The dance has been recorded in Germany, and in Sweden; it survives in France, Italy, Spain, Bohemia and the Balkans. Traces have been discovered on the coasts of the Hebrides and Fifeshire.

The tradition of the Cutler's Sword Dance, performed at Nuremberg in the 14th century, has been preserved in picture and by description. The Sword Dance of the Swedes and the Goths was described by Oleus Magnus in 1555. His description would be apt for any of the surviving Yorkshire dances already mentioned. This particular mid-winter custom serves to remind us how our various English dance traditions have been derived from many different sources. In North-east England the invaders who harried our shores and kept an army of occupation up to the line of the Dane Law left behind the Yorkshire dialect and the Danish place-names, linking us directly with certain of our European kin of a thousand years ago. They also bequeathed a dance drama which throws much light on other traditional customs.

The reader may have noticed that the Grenoside Captain carries a curved sabre—a weapon not suited to the linked-up type of Sword Dance. He represents a different type of sword-bearer, whose office it was to clear a space and to drive away all influences likely to weaken the magic of the ritual ceremony. The function of 'making room' was even more important than the actual implement used for the purpose. There are examples of folk ceremonies which begin with sweeping the floor with a broom or besom. There are processions led by a man with a whip. But the sword-bearer occurs more frequently, and has survived into civic processions in many countries. At

Bampton one of the Morris 'characters' is a sword-bearer, who is also the custodian of the sacred cake, fragments of which he sells to the bystanders throughout the Festival Day. The only function that the sword now fulfils is to bear upon its broad hilt the cake baked from the corn grown in the local fields. This cake, with its magical significance of prosperity and fertility, is a dish in the sacramental feast that concluded the Morris-Dance ritual in its more ceremonial days. But the sword has its own significance as a talisman to drive off evil and keep clear the space for the enactment of the ritual. When the sword-bearer flourishes his blade and sweeps it to and fro, it creates a whistling sound, which has given to an active space-clearer the distinctive title of 'Whiffler'.

If the apparent use is only to clear a physical space, there are traditional instances which clearly indicate that he was, in fact, clearing away the evil spirits. Some Whifflers are capable of performing two functions: whiffling their swords, and then making use of the consecrated space for their linked-up Sword Dance.

One Yugoslav version of the Young Men's Dance, known as the Rusalii, begins with a stately example of the Whifflers' rite. Dancing in a wide, open circle, each man springs slowly from foot to foot, kicking up the free leg in the air like a Highland dancer, and sweeping the sword in a wide circle as he turns completely round. At the end of their 'whiffling' dance they link up their swords, but only to form an open chain leaving a single gap between two of their company. The dancers then perform some simple chain figures. Perhaps the gap is left to allow any lurking evil spirits to find a ready exit. Finally it is closed and the dancers perform their circle dance within the purged area.

The Calusari dancers of Rumania, when providing the framework for the resurrection drama acted inside the ring of linked staves, keep the closed-circle formation throughout. While all evil spirits are thus kept at bay, the animal-men believed to represent the neutral forces of Nature—neither good nor evil—leap over the barrier or creep underneath it just as they like. The actors proper may only enter or leave 'the stage' if a gap is opened for them. There are several examples of the gapped circle dance in Europe. In Fenestrelle in Italy, and the Festival of Les Olivettes in Provence the dancers perform their chain Sword Dance with a gap left open throughout the dance. So do the dancers in the Island of Papa Stour in Shetland. In the English Sword Dances I know of only one surviving example which starts with a deliberately open gap—the Sword Dance of Handsworth, already mentioned. Here the dancers form up in a U-formation, all facing the presence, standing motionless while the music strikes up. Then at the very first step of the dance they bridge the gap and all prance around, 'whiffling' their swords, before they turn inwards to perform the ceremonial clash. The brandish or 'whiffle', however, occurs in several other Yorkshire Sword Dances.

* * * *

The implements now used by the Northumberland and Yorkshire sword dancers have departed somewhat from the orthodox type of sword, and it seems clear that whatever the original dance implement may have been, it has, in process of time, been replaced by trade implements and other means of linkage which came conveniently to hand according to the occupation of the dancers. The Flamborough fishermen dance with a wooden 'sword', held throughout in the left hand, and this wooden slat is used as the link between dancer and dancer while they weave the various patterns and figures. There is good reason to believe that this 'sword' is a tool which they used for making rope mats— a local trade practised on the beach or in front of the cottages. In their mat-making the wooden tool is known as a 'sword' and used in the left hand to press the woven cords close together, while the shuttle is flung with the right hand through the gap between the sword and the edge of the weave.

The influence of this local trade may also have affected the dance itself, for the figures are all reminiscent of weaving, and go by the name of 'threadling', an apt description of the manner in which the individual dancers thread in and out. But such plaiting designs occur so far back in the history of primitive decoration, and are so widespread in folk custom, that their significance is believed to be connected with fertility or generation. This idea certainly fits in with the indications of fertility symbolism, implicit, and, indeed, often explicit in all the men's ceremonial dances. Phallic representations abound in the more primitive European rituals, and they also occur in some English traditions, although not in a very obvious form. It is, of course, only too easy to read into folk custom symbolism which may not be there at all, but the picture of the Winter and Spring dance customs would be quite incomplete were the fertility signs and significances to be omitted or under-estimated. Some

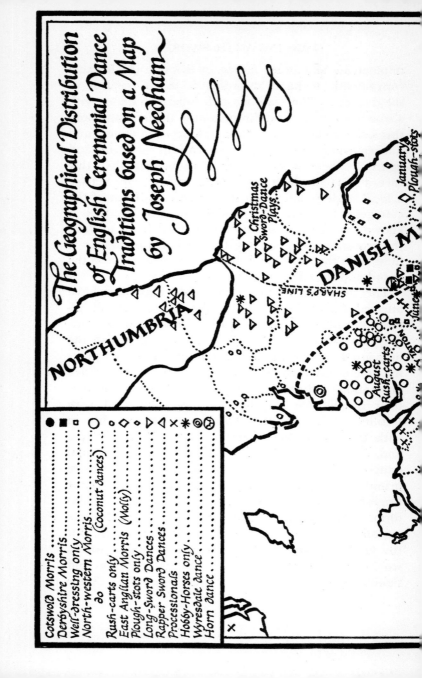

The Geographical Distribution of English Ceremonial Dance Traditions based on a Map by Joseph Needham

NORTHUMBRIA

DANISH M...

Christmas Sword-Dance Plays.

SHARP'S LINE

January Plough-stots

August Rush-carts

Cotswold Morris .... ●
Derbyshire Morris .... ■
Well-dressing only .... ▫
North-western Morris .... ○
      do   (Coconut dances) .. ○
Rush-carts only .... ∘
East Anglian Morris (Molly) .... ◇
Plough-stots only .... ◊
Long-Sword Dances .... ▷
Rapper Sword Dances .... ◁
Processionals .... ✕
Hobby-Horses only .... ✳
Wyresdale dance .... ◎
Horn dance .... ✆

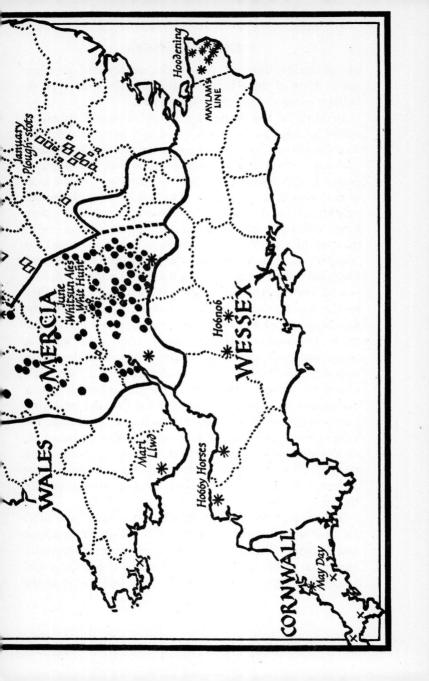

of the fertility symbols have been sublimated to other uses. One of these is the spoon or ladle, now used to collect money from the spectators.

In some of the Yorkshire 'Long' Sword Dances, so called in contrast to the shorter implement used by the Northumbrian dancers, the swords are made of steel, and taper to a fairly sharp point. But the point is pierced, and through the hole is threaded a short loop of coloured braid or ribbon, which is held firmly by the neighbouring dancer. This loop provides a more flexible linkage than is the case if the actual steel end is grasped in the palm of the hand. The short sword, or 'rapper' as it is called in the Northumberland and Durham Sword Dances, has a handle at either end, and one of these is free to rotate, giving greater flexibility to the wrist movements of the dancers. This Northumbrian rapper has evidently been adapted from some trade implement. It has been compared with a scutching-knife, used for scutching flax, and the name 'rapper' may well have been derived from 'scraper', although some authorities have regarded it as a corruption of 'rapier'. The short flexible and bendable instrument has affected the character of the dance, for it brings the performers, now usually five in number, close together in a compact set, and at the same time enables them to execute close intricate designs, very different from the more open-work patterns of the Yorkshire dance.

This 'Short' Sword Dance, which has been practised for centuries by the coal-miners of Northumberland and Durham, has almost completely lost its dramatic incidents. One or two have preserved the 'calling-on' song, in which each dancer is described as an actor and given a fictitious character to indicate disguise. In addition to the Captain who sings the song, may also be found that other universal stock character, the Man-Woman. In the Northumbrian dances she commonly goes by the name of the 'Besom Betty' or the 'Dirty Bet'. She sometimes enters the ring of dancers and puts her bonneted head through the centre of the 'Lock'. There is no longer any scene of a ritual death and resurrection, but there is sufficient residue of the ancient ceremony for the student to relate this dance to the mid-winter ritual. Perhaps the most noticeable difference between the Northumbrian dance and its Yorkshire counterpart, apart from the length and nature of the sword, is the emphasis that has been placed on the step-dance. Clogs have, until recent years, been common wear in the North of England, and to wear a clog is to be half-way towards being a tap-dancer.

In the case of the Grenoside dance, the team always wears clogs, and they do much more stepping than in any of the other Yorkshire dances. In Handsworth, only a few miles away, clogs are no longer worn, and while the style of the dancing depends very much on the ankle boots and leggings, there is no 'step-dancing'.

In Northumbria the 'stepping' has developed recently into a highly polished art, but the clogs have been dropped. The dancers now wear a light shoe or slipper which taps out a deft patter. This 'stepping' occurs at such frequent intervals in the dance that an accomplished Northumbrian sword dancer must first learn to be a competent step dancer.

The divorce of the Sword Dance from its dramatic context has become complete in the case of the North Skelton dance. Now there are two distinct customs.

One is the Christmas Mummers' Play, and the other is the Sword Dance. The North Skelton dance has its characters, the Clown (or Squire) and the Betty. The Betty enters the ring and puts her head through the 'Lock'. There is a mock decapitation and she falls down, but there is no singing and no dialogue.

The Christmas Mummers' Play, in which some of the local Sword Dance team play a part, has a death in it, but this death is not compassed by the sword Lock, but by one of the stock characters stumbling off the back of the Hobby Horse. The Mummers' Play, without any sword dancing, survives widespread as village custom. It deserves some mention here, although it has no dance connected with it and although there is good reason to think that it is a comparatively recent intrusion into the folk-customs of Britain. This danceless play is based on a published version, printed in London in the 16th century, and called 'The Seven Champions of Christendom', produced by a writer named Richard Johnson. From its wide distribution it must have been in the repertory of travelling theatrical companies, and by them was introduced into the country districts. Johnson's written play was sufficiently like the ancient Plough Monday Folk Play to be welcomed and adopted as an acceptable novel variant. The derivatives of Johnson's Play, which we now speak of as 'Mummers' Play', having established themselves as independent forms of country entertainment, deprived the Sword Dance ceremony of half its appeal. While the Sword Dance continued to give pleasure to performers and audience alike, the old ritual drama and dialogue, as it lost its meaning, withered away. The few cases of survival which have been recorded contain a more significant relic of our early history than the popular entertainment that superseded it.

Although the dramatic action and dialogue of the Mummers' Play is of slight interest and significance, the Mummers themselves have managed to preserve the impersonal manner of the more ancient ceremony, and some have even preserved the ritual costume, designed to act as a mask and as a disguise. The Marshfield Paper Boys, whose annual performance in their village in Gloucestershire, may properly be regarded as a traditional festival, derive their name from the peculiar head-dress of finely divided paper streamers which covers them from tip to toe, and through which they have to peer in order to see the other actors. Although their present dialogue is based on the Richard Johnson print, this group of village actors preserve a popular custom which leads right back to the observances of pagan times.

V

Distribution

THE geographical distribution of the different types of
dance throughout the country is of great interest.
In describing the English Morris Dance I have referred
more particularly to one type of dance confined to a
small area in the very heart of England—the concentration being greatest in the Cotswolds. One
Oxfordshire village, Kirtlington, seems to have been
the centre and meeting-place for many of the local
Morris teams. It had its custom, called 'The Lamb
Ale', which included a ceremonial feast and, of course,
a good deal of friendly drinking. It has been suggested by many authorities that the spread of the
Cotswold type of Morris from such a centre as Kirtlington would account for the radial distribution in the
Cotswold area and for its complete absence outside a
radius of fifty or sixty miles from the centre. The fact,
too, that many of the villages which preserved the
custom had local ceremonial feasts, sometimes called
'Lamb Ales' and sometimes 'Whitsun Ales', suggests
the adoption of a custom spreading from one original
source. One investigator (Dr. J. Needham) who, as a
result of dancing with a team in the Cotswold villages,
became deeply interested in the origins and history of
the Morris, devoted a considerable study to this question of distribution, and the result of his research

was published in the *Journal of the E.F.D.S.* He lists
105 examples of the Cotswold Morris village teams
which have been recorded as surviving after 1800.
Many of these have, of course, since died out, but there
are five teams in existence at this moment, or, if they
are not actually dancing, could probably be revived.
The features common to the Cotswold Morris are, a
team of six dancers, wearing bells and using kerchiefs
and, sometimes, sticks in the dance. Their dress is
almost invariably white, studded with coloured decora-
tions, especially ribbons. The accompanying characters are a Fool, or Squire, with a bladder, a Man-
Woman, and a Bagman to take the collection. They
usually appear at Whitsun or on May Day.

The men's dance nearest to this in character, and also
in geography, is the Derbyshire Morris Dance, limited
to that county, and of which there are now only one or
two living examples. The features of this dance are
that the company of dancers may be as many as
twenty in number; there are no bells: they use kerchiefs; the dress is white, decorated with coloured
ribbons, and the characters include a Fool, a Man-
Woman, a King and Queen. They usually appear in
July. The most peculiar feature of this type is that
they dance in two rows. The rows are of different
kinds, with one row wearing what look like women's
hats.

North-west of Derbyshire we have the Lancashire
Morris, associated to some extent with the old Rush-
cart ceremony. The number of dancers varies from
eight to an indefinitely larger number, using sticks, or
slings, constructed of hanks of cotton, or, in one case,
'nuts' fastened upon the hands, knees and waist. Their

season was in August (the time of the Rush Cart and
Rush-bearing Festival). The dancers have already
been described. (See p. 47.)

The fact that all these three types of dance—Cotswold, Derbyshire and Lancashire—are called 'Morris'
is not in itself sufficient reason to regard them as having
a common history and deriving from a common source.
But if we regard the three groups as one, and compare
them with the hilt-and-point Sword Dances of Yorkshire and Northumbria, we notice at once a very
interesting fact regarding their distribution. In his
examination of the Sword-Dance tradition, Needham
lists fifty-seven different Sword Dances as having been
alive in 1800, but only a handful survive in Yorkshire
and in Northumberland to-day. I have already
described the association of the hilt-and-point Sword
Dance with the Plough Monday custom, and if we
regard the two as being part of a common ceremonial,
the distribution of the individual localities where it
has been described, or still survives, shows that Sword
Dance and Plough Play are concentrated in a definite
belt running from north to south. A significant point
is that there is no overlapping between the Sword
Dances in one belt and the various types of Morris
Dance in the other. The name 'Morris' unfortunately
only confuses the picture, for it has been, and still is,
applied indiscriminately to very different kinds of
dancing. Nevertheless, the Morris Dances of the
Cotswolds, Derbyshire and Lancashire have more in
common with each other than any of these have with
the Sword Dances in the other belt. To find anything
like these 'Morris' dancers, with their white clothes
and bells, we have to move outside England altogether,

10. Northumberland Sword Dancers (Beadnell), with Besom Betty. In the background, Cecil Sharp and George Butterworth (collectors).

11. A Yorkshire Sword Dance from Grenoside.

12. A Yorkshire Sword Dance from Handsworth.

13. The Fishermen's Sword Dance from Flamborough Head.

first to Perth in Scotland, where the Glover Incorporation has preserved a similar type of dance until about
1800, and then to Ireland, where there are surviving
fragments of old Celtic processional dances. On the
Continent one finds numerous examples of this 'Morris'
in Yugoslavia, Rumania, Austria, Bohemia, Southern
France and Northern Spain—the white clothes, the
bells and the whole atmosphere of the dance are such
that it could be translated straight to the Cotswolds and
fit immediately into that English scene.

To look for other examples of the Sword Dance one
has to go right out of England, jump clean over Scotland up to the Shetlands or across to Europe. There
is not the slightest trace of it in the South or West of
England. There are small indications of it in the
North of Ireland, and possible vestiges of it in the Kingdom of Fife. Such a peculiar distribution of custom is
too striking to be accepted merely as chance survival.
Needham, in illustration of his article, includes a map
(see p. 72), showing the division of England into the
old kingdoms of Northumbria, Wessex and Mercia, the
latter being divided into the Danish and Saxon parts.
The three types of Morris Dance all fall within the area
of Saxon Mercia. I have already described how the
Sword Dances all fall into the Danish part. Most
authorities are of the opinion that the three types of
Morris described above were part of a custom indigenous
in England long before the advent of the Saxons. The
dances must, therefore, in their opinion, be relics of
either Roman/British, or Keltic, or of pre-Keltic
culture. The fact that the several hundred Cotswold
Morris traditions are closely concentrated upon Kirtlington does not necessarily mean a dissemination from

F

a single centre, but rather indicates the survival of a habit common to the members of the ancient race that first permanently settled in these parts. Whether Keltic or the still older Iberian, the Cotswold Morris claims as its near relations the dances now found in other Keltic regions and in the Iberian peninsula. The three types of Morris were probably an integral part of local custom when the Saxons appeared on the scene and settled down to live side by side with the peoples they found there. But the Saxons may never have adopted the dances.

Quite another story may lie behind the hilt-and-point Sword Dance. So far as England is concerned, it must have been brought to these shores by the people who last colonised Danish Mercia. Our early history bears testimony to the frequency of Viking raids. The Viking stronghold at Flamborough Head, a natural line of defence, is still almost as Danish as it is English. The speech of the fishermen is easy to understand while you are on shore—it seems just a salt-water version of the Yorkshire dialect—but step into one of their Viking-shaped cobles, and their speech becomes unintelligible; for the words connected with their trade, with the sea and the boats are Danish. The Flamborough fishermen have their own Sword Dance, to which I have already referred, and although the various Sword Dances may vary considerably in detail, they all share the peculiar character that the dancers are linked up hilt-and-point. The Shetland dance at Papa Stour must also be Scandinavian in origin, for the people of those islands are pure Nordic. The traces of the dance found in Fife and on the North coast can also be explained in terms of Scandinavian influence, for to the old sea-raiders no part of the coastline was immune.

When Cecil Sharp first began investigating these two types of men's ceremonial dance, he inclined to the view that one was derived from the other. He regarded the Sword Dance as the older because of its close relation with the ritual Folk Play, and he derived the sticks and kerchiefs used by the Morris dancers from the swords. Possibly, if one could go back far enough in pre-history, the mid-winter Sword Dance with the Plough Play, and the Young Men's Dance of Lent and Whitsuntide, might converge. We might then find the original actors engaged in a continuous ritual like that of Malekula, turning the old year into the new, banishing evil and quickening the good life with their songs and dances. But before accepting any such hypothesis the reader should himself browse among the pages of the books given in the bibliography.

VI

Processions

REFERENCE has frequently been made to the stock characters appearing with the Morris dancers and the Sword dancers, and to the fact that these characters also appear as dramatis personæ in the Plough Monday Folk Play and in the Christmas Mummers' Play. Divorced from their play-acting the old actors have continued to hang round the skirts of the dance and to claim a share in the public attention which formerly was theirs by divine right. Here and there, in different parts of England, are other relics which belong to the traditions of our forbears. The Maypole itself still stands, a permanent monument to the pagan past, in a surprising number of places. Other relics make a brief annual appearance to remind us how persistent and how hard to kill is local custom. Seasonal processions, once dance ceremonies but which have now degenerated into a march up the village street or a hike across country, were common up to the outbreak of the 1914 war in Somerset, Sussex, Dorset, Hampshire, Wiltshire and Berkshire. These 'club walks', as they are called, would seem to have been derived from old processional dances. There are indications in one or two of the Wiltshire club walks that at the end of the procession they danced a stationary country dance known as 'Bricks and Mortar'.

The connection of the walk with a club is significant, for the Whitsuntide Morris dancers, both in the Cotswolds and in Derbyshire, were members of clubs of the masonic type, and it was always a matter of club selection before a man could enter the Morris team. The Morris Dance may have been just a part of a procession; the Elected Men going in the van and the rest of the community falling in behind. Such processions have been described in Ireland, including one where the women are segregated in the centre of the procession, the men providing both an advance and a rear guard.

Of the dance processions in England in which the whole community takes part, the most familiar is the Furry Dance of Helston in Cornwall. This procession, performed on the second Saturday in May, is a purification celebration carried out by as many as care to take part. The dancers not only promenade through the streets of the town, but enter the houses on either side and parade through the rooms, sometimes going out of the back door to enter the next house by the back door, and emerging on the street to join the main body of the procession. At one time the dancers in Helston carried sprigs of May blossom or green broom, and used these to brush different objects in the rooms through which they passed. There are similar spring-cleaning processions on the Continent, and the Cornish custom was not always confined to Helston.

The ceremony of the Rush-bearing in the North-west of England, mentioned in connection with the Lancashire Morris Dance, and performed in late August and early September, was not unlike the Helston dance in its character. The object of the ceremony was not only to purge evil after the winter, but to provide the fresh green rushes in the dwellings before the next winter set in.

A peculiar procession has survived in Somerset in the Minehead Hobby Horse, which perambulates the town every year on May Day, visiting various houses on the way. This character has been affected by its proximity to the sea, for it is half animal and half boat. A far more active Hobby Horse appears on the first of May at Padstow in Cornwall. He must not only perambulate the streets, but go through a recurring cycle of death and resurrection repeated every few minutes. Spurred on by another character called the 'club-man', the Hobby Horse dances and capers among the excited onlookers, to the music of accordion and drum. Suddenly the music stops, its caperings cease, and the 'animal-man' sinks to the ground as the musicians and onlookers close in and sing a dirge. The club-man crouches and strokes the Horse's nose with his club, while the dirge continues. It stops and the dance-music strikes up again. Club-man and Horse leap high in the air and prance about as actively as before. Here we meet the death and resurrection theme in its most concentrated form. The Padstow Horse is far more like an African medicine-man than the conventional Hobby Horse. But for the tiny horse's head and the tail, the medicine-man would not be taken for a horse at all. The dancer who plays the part of the Horse stands inside a circular framework slung from his neck, measuring in diameter nearly 4 feet. Over this hoop-like structure, stretching from his neck to the ground, is a covering of canvas, blacked with liquid tar. Topping the dancer's head and ending in a high conical hat is a grotesque mask, decorated and coloured with all the violent imagination of an African savage. While the Horse is capering and swirling, the onlookers dance round it, shouting and laughing—some not a little frightened. Occasionally the Horse manages to get a young girl right under the skirt. Such an adventure, or even a smear of wet tar on face or garments, is a safeguard against all evil for the next twelve months.

The Hobby Horse is an old pagan character with its own geographical distribution. In England it belonged just as much to the Morris Dance as to the Sword Dance. It also has strongholds in places where neither Sword nor Morris survive, nor ever had a foothold. In the extreme south-east corner of Kent, the Hooden Horse still appears. This species is constructed from a horse's skull stuck on the end of a pole, which is carried by a dancer hooded by a white sheet or other covering. Such a 'Hobby' was known in Dorset, Hampshire and Wiltshire, as well as in Somerset and Cornwall. It is still remembered in Wales and in Ormskirk, Lancashire.

In South Yorkshire and in Derbyshire the place of 'Old Hoss' is taken by the 'Old Tup'. Except for the head being sheep instead of horse, the ritual remains much the same. I am indebted to my friend, Colonel Eustace Smith, for a description of the Old Tup, which annually visited his kitchen in South Yorkshire at Christmas-time. The company are seated, enjoying games and dances, which are interrupted by the entry of Old Tup, to smell out the defaulters. Old Tup is asked who has been mean over the last church collection, who has failed to pay his income tax, which is the girl who kicks off her bed-clothes when she dreams of her sweetheart, and similar jibes based upon local gossip. Old Tup, after a preliminary sniff round his audience, selects some unfortunate person, who at once becomes the butt of the hilarious company.

Whether the chosen animal was horse or sheep (and it is easy to see why the sheep should belong to Derbyshire and the horse to Kent), the real point of the ceremony was to give the animal-man a chance to show his powers. The fact that one animal-man performs his magic at Christmas-time and another does his act of death and resurrection on the first of May, does not worry the student of folk-lore. These ancient festivals have, in any case, been shifted away from their original dates by the changes in the calendar. Any custom that occurs between Christmas and May might claim a link with the ceremonies of the Spring equinox.

One peculiar relic of pre-Christian days which has shifted its date in comparatively recent times is the Horn Dance of Abbots Bromley, in Staffordshire. Here in one ritual we find our friends the stock characters of the Man-Woman, the Fool, the Hobby Horse and the six elected men dancers: in this case the Morris Men represent forest stags. The whole company make a countryside perambulation lasting all day. The perambulation is carried out once a year: it starts from the door of the parish church and ends in a club feast at one of the oldest hostelries in the ancient town. The six Morris Men each bear upon their shoulders a set of antlers, three of which are painted black and three white. They lead the procession, the three black preceding the three white, and the other characters follow in the order of the Fool, the Maid Marian, the Hobby Horse and a boy carrying a cross-bow and an arrow. Their normal method of processing is to trot in Indian file, the leader of the 'blacks' making curious serpentine loops and challenging the three 'whites'. When the leader desires to perform the stationary set dance, he merely rounds the chain off into a circle, flattens it into two files of five dancers each, thus bringing the three white horns opposite the three black. The set dance is a symbolic fight between these two groups of protagonists. They advance, retire and cross sides. It looks realistic enough as the great sets of horns are swung down and up as the bearers lunge forward at each other. After the set dance the leader simply casts off or goes forward, while all tail on behind in single file in their usual order. Throughout the procession the boy with the bow and arrow shoots his weapon at the leading stag. The Hobby Horse, which is of the more conventional kind, has a hinged lower jaw so that it can snap and clatter in time with the rhythm of the dance. The music is now provided by a melodeon and triangle.

Various local accounts are given of the origin and history of the dance, but this local information is very incomplete. Such a relic of pre-history can only be understood and interpreted by implication and by reference to the folk ritual and barbaric rites of other peoples. Although called a Morris Dance, it has been classified variously as a hunting dance, a fertility rite, and a contest between good and evil—between life and death. All these elements seem to lurk behind the pageantry. The fertility element is probably the dominant one to the student of folk-lore, who recognises the two wooden implements carried by the Maid Marian as crude representations of the male and female principles. The local farmers certainly connect the Horn-running with fertility, for they regard it as a piece of bad luck if the Horn dancers miss their farms in any particular year. It was a fortunate occurrence for its preservation that this ancient ritual should have been adopted by the local church. The history of the early Church in England makes frequent reference to the tolerance to be shown to the old pagan customs of the people. Some were successfully digested into the Christian Festivals. Others gradually died out as belief in their value faded. This particular custom at Abbots Bromley has been safeguarded by adoption by the church. The Vicar is the custodian of the horns, which hang in the vestry throughout the year. If it had not been for such safeguard, it is almost certain that so primitive a ceremony and so interesting a dance could not have survived. It is the only dance of its kind in England, and indeed, in Europe.

VII

The First Actor

AT this point it is necessary to turn our attention to the character who, in the Abbots Bromley procession, dressed as a jester, trots behind the six deer/men. The court jester of feudal times is a meaningless figure by himself. We must look to his antecedents if we are to appreciate his importance. Tracing back is not merely a question of going backward in time. Some of his functions are revealed in other folk-dance customs still alive. The Fool as an upsetter of conventional behaviour can be recognised in the Lord of Misrule who presided at the Feast of Fools, a mediæval custom to which some attention has been given in literature. As a maker of magic and medicine-man, he has already been described as the Green Man. As scapegoat and redeemer he can be identified in the Robin Hood, or Robin-of-the-Wood, who has to bleed to death, and as the chief character in the Revesby Play who is 'killed' by his six sons.

Although the Robin Hood of folk tradition bears the mark of a one-time pagan god and scapegoat, there is some evidence, as Sir Edmund Chambers and others have shown, of the actual existence of the historical character who excelled at the long bow and who waged a private war with the Sheriff of Nottingham. Even that Robin Hood, according to the ballads and tales, was soundly thrashed by Little John, the Potter and others, so mixed are the literary and folk traditions. Possibly the tangle may be unravelled by exhaustive research in the two realms of folk-lore and literature. I have a personal leaning toward a connection between the Hood of Robin and the Hood of the Hooden Horse as the masks disguising the actor–scapegoat playing his ancient role.

The unfortunate scapegoats who are beaten and trounced for the good of the community are recurrent figures in folk-lore, and most of them are padded to take the shrewd blows of the crowd. The grotesque and mis-shapen figures in the Shrove Tuesday festival at Binches in Belgium, who jig up and down to ring the great cow-bells hung on their waists, have to sustain a fuselade of oranges. The oranges they catch and throw back to the crowd, but the missiles were not always so soft and yielding. The costume of the Morris dancers of the Glover's Incorporation in Perth, one specimen of which is still preserved in the Glover's Museum, was so constructed that it could be padded out. Local tradition has it that these local Morris dancers were subject to a bombardment of missiles, including broken glass. The characters in the Folk Plays in the Balkan Peninsula are all padded. In our own degenerate versions of the Folk Play the persistence of the scapegoat is seen in the entrance of Hump-backed Jack, who carries his family upon his back. Punchinello of the Comedia Del Arte, and our own Mr. Punch, are direct descendants of this mis-shapen scapegoat.

To delve farther into the background of the Fool involves reference to the traditions of other peoples and to the customs of native tribes at an earlier stage in evolution from primitive society. The king of the sacred grove, destined to be killed by his successor, who furnished the starting point for Sir James Fraser's tremendous investigations which he subsequently published in 'The Golden Bough', is an ancestor of the folk Fool. Priests and kings of all kinds are related to him. His story is so involved and complicated that it embraces a vast portion of the history of man, from the moment he emerges as distinct from the animals.

The Fool in the Morris Dance doubles the part of leader or Squire with that of Clown or entertainer. As Squire he manages the club and maintains its membership and its standard of dancing. As the Clown he contrives to bridge the gap between dancers and spectators and to make the latter feel that they are participators and as essential as the performers. It is curious how much influence a good Clown has on both parties. No doubt it is the usefulness of this connecting function that in part explains the attachment to the Morris and Sword Dances of the stock characters who no longer have a dialogue to speak nor a part to act. The aspect of the Fool which made him a valued member of a great feudal household, gave him power to dispel gloom and to raise spirits, and found him a part in so many of Shakespeare's plays, is his interpretation of the irrational side of life. To be silly in the mediæval sense meant to be holy and sensitive to religious impulse.

The outstanding function of the Fool in folk-lore is to undergo death and revival. The scholars identify him with the Sun God and the cult of Osiris of Egypt. This interpretation finds much supporting evidence in the Sword Dances of England, Germany, Austria and other parts of Europe. The Lock of swords, whether composed of from five or more weapons, makes a circular pattern and repeats sun symbols pictured by man in the stages of the march to civilisation. This Lock is not only held aloft by the Captain in the Sword Dance, but, in certain cases, is made to rotate sun-wise over the heads of the ring of dancers. In the Revesby Play dialogue the Lock is spoken of as a looking-glass, and the Fool describes how to see himself in it and how, if he has to die, he will die with his face to the light for all. Looking-glasses are used to decorate the Jack-in-the-Green and the head-gear of Morris dancers.

One aspect of the Fool, implicit in nearly all surviving ritual dances, is that of the initiate. In the Schemenlaufen or ghost-running ceremonies of Bohemia, which have been described by Dr. Richard Wolfram, the word 'Fool' is applied to all the performers, all of whom are initiates. Once admitted into the special society which was devoted to the maintenance of the ritual, they are entitled to privileged behaviour. They express this, naturally, by seeking to do what is the opposite of convention. It is this aspect of the privileged initiate which distinguished the curious custom of the Lord of Misrule, and of the Boy Bishop, who, during his short tenure of office, was allowed and encouraged to do just what he liked. The interpretation of the Fool as an initiate is applicable, therefore, to all the actors who take part in a Sword Dance or Folk Play, and, indeed, to all the members of a Morris side. As William Wells says of his Morris team at Bampton, as he scratches his fiddle and calls the team into formation—'Here we are: six Fools and one dancer!'

A similar view of that of Wolfram was taken by Kurt Meschke, who, in a comprehensive examination of German Sword Dances, was inclined to regard all Sword Dances as of German origin. The Italian Sword Dances of Piedmont, and the French Sword Dances in the Dauphiné and Provence, apart from the English and Shetland revivals in our own country, indicate clearly that the dance belonged to a culture wider than that exercised by the Teutonic race. The Sword Dance in the Dauphiné, which is called the Baccubert, is believed to be of Celtic origin, and I think now one can say fairly confidently that the hilt-and-point Sword Dance as a ritual must have belonged to Indo-European culture. The Mahrout Indians have the dance and they are as much like English Sword dancers as any of the Teutonic groups which Meschke mentions in his book.

There is one link between the Sword Dance of Provence, Piedmont and the Dauphiné on the one hand, with the Morris Dance of the Calusari on the other. Both sets of dancers carry a maypole. A circular dance is performed round this pole by the Fools, and in the case of the Calusari this dance is part of the actual initiation at the very beginning of their seasonal rite. We have here a connection, also, with the Abram Lancashire Morris Dance performed round 'the Bush'. The relation of this bush or pole symbol of living vegetation to the young men initiated into the mystery is a theme which seems quite universal in pre-Christian dance ritual.

The Baccubert dancers of the Dauphiné number nine, eleven or thirteen, as do the Calusari, and they have other elements in common. Yet the two dances are as different in apparent nature and style as it would be possible to conceive—the Rumanian dance being a thing of passion which throbs from start to finish, while the French is a dignified, deliberate affair with all the solemnity of a church ceremony. Because of this difference, and owing to the fact that one dance is performed with staves and the other with swords, folk-lore experts are apt to place them in separate specific classes, as I have, indeed, done myself, under the labels of 'Sword Dance' and 'Morris Dance'. A comparative study carried over a sufficiently wide field would, in my view, tend to show that in essence they derive from one original source.

15. The Minehead Hobby Horse.

14. The Royal Earsdon Sword Dancers
(Northumberland), showing the Lock.

16. The Padstow Hobby Horse with Teaser or Club-Man.

VIII

The Community Dances

THE peasantry of Europe, long after they were converted to Christianity, continued to observe many of their old country customs, despite their pagan origin and dedication to Gods long since renounced. Some customs already described depended upon a small select body of men. On other occasions the whole community took a part in the celebrations. Out of the community celebrations grew a form of social dance which has continued through the centuries to our own times. This community dance of the country people is found in some form or other in every country in Europe. It takes many forms, ranging from the great circle of divers dancers, down to the smallest unit of two couples. The essence of its character is that the individual loses his 'self' in the common bond of unanimous expression, and that the social element of give-and-take is paramount. The community dance must have originated in a number of different ways, and possibly arose out of a number of different seasonal rites. The longways, or long dance, is, in Europe, perhaps the most common form. The chain or round is probably as old or even older. The round is inseparable from the Whitsuntide May Day and other Spring festivals, when the community perambulated round some object such as a sacred grove or tree, or

G

97

later, the church. In England it is coupled with the Maypole. Although it was confined to such a special celebration as the May Day Festival, the nature of the country dance has made it a suitable means of revelry at all moments of good fortune and happiness. Thomas Hardy's description of the country dance at a village wedding in 'Under The Greenwood Tree' is probably as clear a picture of the English country dance in recent times as we can expect to find. It reflects the simple nature of the country people, their naturalness, good manners and gaiety.

The peasantry as a distinct English class have been dead this hundred years, and the countryman of to-day is a very different individual from the peasant forbear, descended in the direct line from the earliest cultivators of our soil. The peasant dance outlived the peasantry and still persists. For a considerable period it enjoyed a fashionable patronage, and it has been influenced from time to time by the fashionable beings who came out of the towns. Itinerant fiddlers must constantly have hawked the country dance-tunes from county to county, and the peasants themselves have brought their rustic dancing into the great cities.

Very little is known historically about the Country Dance and its origins. In mediæval days it was no doubt just taken for granted as part of the country life, for the earliest literature available makes no direct mention of it until the beginning of the 16th century. At that time, among the royal palaces and the houses of the great, the social dances were imported French and Italian dances, some of them, no doubt, going back to the Norman Conquest. It was not until the reign of Henry the Seventh that we find occasional references to the dances of the common people. These first find mention as novelties in the popular Tudor entertainment, the Court Masque. In 1510 Henry the Eighth staged an elaborate Masque in which, for the first time, we find the Robin Hood Games—a sophisticated form of Folk Play—mentioned.

In Elizabeth's reign it seems that the peasant dance had established itself at Court as an informal pastime. It was probably much more suited to the robust Elizabethans than the stately Pavane and other courtly French and Italian dances, of which they were, by this time, growing tired. The Masques were growing in popularity as indoor entertainment, and foremost among the enthusiasts were the members of the Inns of Court. Grays Inn particularly seems to have acquired a highly talented team of amateur performers, and there is a specific reference to a Country Dance they performed at Court when they presented their Masque there in 1613.

During the next forty years the popularity of the English dance of the countryside must have spread far and wide, for in 1650 was published a handbook clearly aimed at a public already familiar with that kind of dancing and versed in its characteristic movements. John Playford was a bookseller and a musician of considerable ability. He owned a shop at the corner of the Inner Temple, where he sold books of tunes and other musical publications. His little handbook on Country Dances he called 'The English Dancing Master—Plaine and Easie Rules for the Dancing of Country Dances, with the Tunes to each Dance'. The title-page bears the endorsement that it was printed by Thomas Harper, and to be sold by

John Playford at his shop in the Inner Temple, near
the church door, 1651. Actually this date is an error,
for the handbook was issued in 1650 : evidently a
rushed affair—perhaps to anticipate a competitor. The
book contains rather more than one hundred dances in
various formations, ranging from the simple progressive
round, through the set rounds and squares for eight, to
the little longways groups of three and four couples,
and, of course, including the long dance 'for as many as
will'. This handbook must have won instant popularity, for the first edition was succeeded by others
issued at frequent intervals during the next hundred
years, and was continued by John Playford's successors
very much in the form of the original. In each edition
some of the old dances are repeated, but there are
always a large number of new forms introduced. A
comparison of the various editions shows that original
dances, which may have been recently brought in
from the countryside, were gradually supplanted by
creations which, although keeping to the forms of the
original dances, rapidly changed in manner, content
and character as the dancing-masters moulded the
material to make it more suited to their professional
needs. Gradually the old rounds and squares are
ousted by the longways or 'contra dances'. These,
with their two straight lines of men and women, provided the dancing-master with a vulnerable company
which he drilled and groomed like recruits on the
barrack square.

To the musicians of this time Country Dances were
by no means small fry, for they were quite ready to
accept a commission for the composition of a new dance-
tune. Playford himself may have made such contribu-

tions to his own early editions. Certainly he had musical friends who may have helped him to gather his material, and even to compile his book. Mr. Parsons and Mr. Confess were probably responsible for some of the pages, for both are preserved for posterity in Country Dances which bear their names. When a new dance was composed at some great house, it might take the name of the house or of the noble Lord or Lady who commissioned the work. Apley House, Sion House, Slaughter House and Hunsdon House all gave their names to Country Dances, and 'My Lady Winwood's Maggot', 'My Lord of Carnarvon's Jig', 'My Lady Foster's Delight' and 'Lady Banbury's Hornpipe', preserve the names of a few of the patrons of the social entertainment of the day.

In spite of Playford's handbook and the various editions of 'The Dancing Master', we know really very little as to how these dances were actually performed. The instructions tell you what to do, but they do not tell you how to do it. Some of the dances in the early editions may have retained the rustic character of the peasant originals, but the majority of them must, so far as we can be guided by the music to which they were wedded and by the costumes worn by the gentry of the period, have been both stately and sophisticated. In the successive editions the tunes lose their dance jigginess and grow more and more song-like and lyrical. Very few of them can pass as a folk-tune. Indeed, this could hardly be otherwise if we reflect that conscious minds were working to produce conscious efforts. Although the music is not 'folk', much of it is supremely beautiful, and clearly comes from the hand of fine composers, some of them men of genius, including Henry Purcell.

All the time that this fashionable social dance was growing away from its rustic origin, the original itself continued to delight people in the country places. No doubt at times one of these traditional Country Dances would be imported into a ballroom, bringing with it a breath of fresh air, and temporarily influencing the pose of the assembly and its manner of dancing. Contrariwise, at times the peasantry may have acquired a novelty from Town, bringing in a touch of conscious sophistication to smooth the rugged manners of the village green. There is evidence of much give-and-take between Town and Country in many forms of popular recreation ever since the beginning of Elizabeth's reign.

Although much is made of the banning of the Maypoles by the Puritans, and their re-introduction at the time of the Restoration, the customs of the peasantry were largely unaffected by the Civil War, as they have been unaffected by all wars including those of our own time. The home-made dances of the countryside furnished the basis for village parties right on to the present day. Individual dances, no doubt, had their vogue and died out, but on the whole, country people enjoy most the old familiar forms. The gentry were avid for dance novelties. The peasantry held fast to the old dances that had 'come out of the ground'. Some of these old rustic Country Dances that were patronised and enjoyed an ephemeral popularity in Town life, winning a page in Playford's book, lingered on in the countryside, long after their Town equivalent had died. There is the case of 'Hunt

the Squirrel'. This dance grew from an old ceremonial, like the hunting of the Wren in the Isle of
Man. 'Hunt the Squirrel', with its old tune, found its
way into the ballrooms in Elizabethan or Stuart days,
then evidently fell out of fashion. Yet this was one of
the dances, still with its ancient melody, that Cecil
Sharp noted in a Warwickshire village 250 years
later.

The country people never lost their love of these
old social set dances. From Cornwall to the Border
Counties, and into Scotland, they survive in rural
districts, particularly in Northern England. The old
reels, jigs and hornpipes still set pulses tingling and feet
tapping. Furthermore, they have the power to stir
the blood of many a modern sophisticate. It is no
wonder that so many old dances and songs have been
found preserved far from their native source. Generations of voluntary exiles have treasured these links which
bind them to their native land and to one another.
My grandfather, David Kennedy, a world traveller in
Scots songs, found his richest rewards among the small
Scottish communities in distant lands.

It is not only the Scots who yearn for their own music,
although they may do so more consciously than other
nations. I remember one occasion in the small remote
township of Yorkton, Saskatchewan, where a team
of dancers gave a performance of the English folk-
dances and songs. Most of the spectators had never
seen England, and none had seen before the dances
we showed, yet many in the audience were moved to
tears and, lest we had been disconcerted by our
reception, despatched several spokesmen to visit our
dressing-rooms to explain that they had cried for joy

because we had given them such longing for the England they had never seen.

Songs and dances that have died out in England persist in overseas communities of English origin. Some have already been brought back from New-foundland, the New England States and the Southern States, and there may be more still to find. In England itself the decline of the village social dance, which went hand in hand with the ebb of country life generally under free trade and imported foodstuffs, was almost complete when Cecil Sharp began to pick up the remaining fragments. He may have expected to find more than he did and have been disappointed with the quantity and quality of those traditional Country Dances he collected. In any case, he was at that time more absorbed in the ceremonial men's dances, and prepared to give them priority. Then his interest was aroused in the dances printed in Playford's book, and for the rest of his life these absorbed him to the exclusion of the living Country Dances. It is no wonder that Sharp was fascinated by the County Dances in Playford's book, once his attention had been drawn to them. The mere problem of deciphering the music and instructions is as absorbing as a crossword puzzle. Once he felt sure he held the key to the code, he systematically transcribed dance after dance, and published them in an easily intelligible form. But he made one specific personal contribution, and that was to give them a modern style of performance, so that they could be of use to the people of the present day. He interpreted the dances in the light of the few surviving traditional Country Dances he had collected, but he advocated steps habitual to young energetic people, such as running and skipping. On such a basis he thought it would be possible for the people of the 20th century to recapture a 17th-century dance.

In actual fact, time has proved that only a few of the Playford Country Dances answer satisfactorily to this athletic treatment. The majority ask for something more sedate and more consciously mannered. They demand a finished performance, like the madrigal, by a group of people possessing a measure of conscious technique. The dances call for controlled gesture, and a developed feeling for movement and music. But those simple dances that have proved their adaptability form a valuable addition to the national repertory. Indeed, they have become an integral part of the inherited tradition of the English, and their names are household words. Who has not heard of Sellenger's Round, of Dargason, Newcastle and Hit and Miss? They and their like have travelled far afield since they first escaped from the dusty leaves of Playford's old manual. People of all colours, living in all continents, have danced them. Recently I noticed two of them figuring in a Californian dance programme, rubbing shoulders with exotic South American couple dances and the North American Square. I mentioned earlier that this latter dance has a story all its own. It is a story that reveals the give and take process between old and new, between Town and Country, and between people and people. If it turns out to be rather long and involved, I hope the reader will follow it patiently, for it serves to illustrate the nature of the changes and chances that have moulded traditional dance and music.

At first sight the Square Dance would appear to be a

direct descendant of the set dances of the 19th century, known in Europe under such titles as the 'Quadrilles', 'Cotillions', 'Lancers' and 'Caledonians'. These ball-room figure dances, which became fashionable in England and Scotland during the 19th century, were imports from France, and for that reason were regarded by the British gentry as chic as well as novel. At the time of their appearance at British Balls and Assemblies, the only Country Dances that had survived were long-ways sets, themselves the descendants of the 17th- and 18th-century dances recorded in the various editions of Playford's 'Dancing Master'. The imported French squares therefore struck a new note, and were accept-able mainly on that ground. But when these same French squares filtered into the United States, they mingled with older traditional square and round dances, introduced in the Colonial days from England, Scot-land and Ireland. What Cecil Sharp found in the Kentucky mountains was the ancient Progressive Round of four or more couples, a real folk-dance con-taining figures from the Rounds and Chains of Tudor days and earlier periods. At the risk of over-simplifying the problem, I should describe the Kentucky dance as essentially an old chain dance, whereas the more recently imported (or French) square dances are essentially non-circular in structure, the patterns being made across the set rather than round it. In New England the local Square Dances are closely akin to the French Squares or Quadrilles. On this argument, a New England Square may be contrasted with a Kentucky Square in terms of 'ballroom' as compared with 'folk' dance. Although such contrast is fairly clear in the comparison of these extreme cases, one finds in other parts of the United States every possible gradation between them.

In the collection of Western Square Dances made by Lloyd Shaw in Colorado, and published by him just before the recent war, are included figures that derive from both sources. The New England quadrilles and the Kentucky chain figures are given side by side as being equally acceptable to the Western Square dancer. Shaw himself perceives that there have been at least two distinct sources, and recognises the chains and progressive figures as representing the older folk tradition. But the Square Set occurs in Europe as an ancient folkdance pattern in many countries, as well as in Britain and France. At an International Festival at Stockholm in 1939, at which practically every country in Europe was represented, some form of Square Dance was presented by nearly every one of the national teams. Some of these squares might have been derived from the French Quadrilles, but the majority were obviously local traditional dances. Since the United States has been receiving immigrants from all parts of Europe for the last hundred years, it is clear that other European 'squares' have been introduced into many localities by these various nationals. The newly imported square figures would, of course, be welcome as new variants to add to the local dance, and there is evidence that in many parts of the United States recently imported Square Dance figures from Europe have been absorbed into this American dance.

The study of the square type of folk-dance is still further complicated by the fact that the Quadrilles, Lancers and other French Squares, popularised in the 19th century, were themselves just French fashionings of a square folk-dance perhaps previously imported from England. Here the traditional square folk-dance persisted in the more remote country places while the imported French Squares of the 19th century were enjoying their relatively brief period of popularity.

The decline in the vogue of the imported French Squares was due to the difficulty of memorising the sequence of movements and the effort required to learn the various patterns. The indigenous Country Dances, although they suffered from this drawback, were saved by their greater simplicity and by the very short sequences of which they are composed.

The success of the American form of the Square Dance is entirely due to an old technique now lost in Europe but retained and developed on the American continent. This technique lifts the responsibility of figure memorising away from the dancer and places it upon the M.C. The American Country Dance M.C. is consequently a much more important figure than a mere controller of programme and floor manners—he may actually compose the dance as it is being performed. The 'Caller', as he is universally known, chants his continuous direction to the whole company, warning them just at the right moment what the next change is going to be, and giving zest to the occasion by his wit and rhythmic syllables. The art of calling, developed out of the more casual reminders of the early European Dancing Masters, is not confined to one part of the United States. Good Callers with clever rhymes and a large repertory of figures and sequences are to be found over the whole area of the North American continent. Even in the Province of Quebec, where the words are French, the method of Calling is American rather than European.

Personally I regard this American Square Dance as part of our own British dance tradition. Cecil Sharp himself paved the way with the Kentucky Running Set, and with the American–English folk-songs. He had no difficulty in convincing folk-song students in both countries that this Mountain music was a common inheritance. America deserves England's gratitude for preserving a treasure which had been very nearly lost in the home country. This holds for the Square and Country Dances that live on the other side. Most of them were derived from these Islands, and are part of the repertoire of England's dances.

IX

Instruments and Tunes

ANIMALS and birds dance silently. Men can also do so. But rhythmic action of a vigorous kind tends to provoke him to shouts and cries. The emotional relation of dance-act to dance-chant is so close that the one can produce the other. One form of vocal accompaniment practised by negro dancers is a tuneless hiss, sounded between the beats. This elemental dance 'music' can be observed in the dance-halls in the Harlem district of New York City. In certain native African dances an addition to this crude singing accompaniment is provided by the dancers beating their chests on the off-beat. The origin of the drum may be found in this dance-gesture of beating the chest. The drum has remained among primitives the favourite dance instrument. Its variation of form is almost infinite, and there is practically no limit to its expressive use for physical music. The part it plays in stimulating the impulse, preserving unanimity and keeping the pulsations alive can be undertaken by many stringed instruments, but these cannot quite reproduce its immediate effect on the solar plexus. The double bass, the banjo, the mandolin, the guitar and the ukelele all have their usefulness as percussion instruments when used to provide a continuous series of throbs. But the dancer requires something more than a mere series of throbs. These must be strung together with a sense of continuity, and bunched to give undulating patterns. The chanting which sustains the physical rhythm can also be reinforced, and even replaced by wind instruments droning on a single note, or by a confused whine caused by two or three notes played by two or three different instruments simultaneously. The pioneer who discovered that he could get a change of note by cutting up different lengths of tube or by boring a finger-hole in the side of a tube, founded a family of wind instruments which have not only played their part in dance accompaniment, but have revolutionised the art of music as well.

In European countries this wind-instrument development seems to have had two starting points, one with the reed or straw, and the other with the soft-wood sapling. The straw pipe and the wooden whistle have both been associated with the traditional dance in Europe. The reed-pipe, in Welsh the Pibgorn, in English the Hornpipe, was for hundreds of years the source of dance-music for the European peasant. It later gave its name to the dance itself. Eventually the name ceased to label an instrument and became identified with a particular kind of tune. In the literature of the 16th century the word 'hornpipe' seems to mean any kind of peasant dance, but it may have referred specifically to the Morris Dance. Later the term was applied to a composed tune reminiscent of the peasant dance. Towards the end of the 17th century it was confined to dance-airs composed in triple time. The lovely Hornpipes of Henry Purcell are of this kind. Later again, having been specifically connected with triple tunes for a hundred years, the term widened its application once more, and eventually has become lodged with a dance measured in 4/4 time, a type of folk-dance tune which has figured in the repertory of the country people throughout historical times.

The linkage of throbbing impulse with sustaining melody must have been made by the European ritual dancers at a very early stage. In simple form it has survived among the Basques and the English Morris dancers. The Spanish Basques and the English players use a combination of three-holed whistle and drum or tambourine, the whistle being played by the left hand, while the tambourine, slung on the left wrist, is beaten by a small stick carried in the right hand. This one-man band evidently sufficed for many hundreds of years. In England the combination was known as the 'pipe and tabor' (pronounced 'tabber'). While there were probably different methods of striking the tabor, a regular way seems to have been to hold the short stick in the middle and, using both ends of it, to beat out a continuous tattoo. This tattoo imparted a tremulous character to the music and to the dance, giving every individual movement a preliminary shake or shiver. This shivering effect, so essential a character of the traditional Morris step, is emphasised by the ringing of the bells fastened to the lower part of the leg.

The Basque version of this ancient dance instrument is called in Spain the Txistu and in France the Tchirula. The Spanish player uses a fairly deep side-drum, the Tamboril, while his French counterpart embraces with his left arm a peculiar percussion instrument consisting of a long, narrow box with four strings stretched right across its mouth and running parallel with the long side. This French substitute for the drum, the

17. The Abbots Bromley Horn Dance.

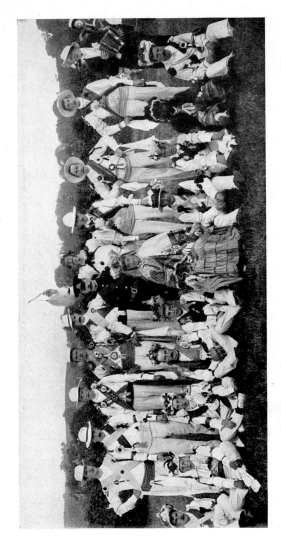

18. The Winster Morris Dancers (Derbyshire): the black face in the front row is the Man–Woman.

Ttun-ttun, is beaten with a flexible, flat stick which hits all four strings at once, producing a sustaining drone, as well as a percussive throb. The ritual folk-dance demands both pulse and drone, or continuo, the pulse giving the dancer his lift while the drone sustains the movement, binding each part to make a whole. Presumably it was to keep the drone going that the piper first introduced an air reservoir in the form of a bag. In its simplest form the bag-pipe consists of a rectangular bag made of goat's skin. A tube is stuck into one corner for the admission of the air. There is another tube with a reed to make the drone, and a third 'keyed' tube to produce the melody—the 'chanter'. The fourth corner goes under the player's arm. Such primitive bag-pipes are common in Eastern Europe. In Western Europe the bag-pipe has been developed to a considerable degree. In the case of the Highland war-pipes three large drones play a continuous chord. In the Northumbrian pipes there are three different instruments—the Long Pipe, the Half Long and the Small. The Longs are blown by mouth, but the Small pipe is blown by bellows strapped to the player's waist and activated by the right arm, while the bag which the bellows inflate is held under his left arm. The Irish dance-pipes, which are also blown with the bellows, are so complicated that they require the player to sit with the pipes resting across his knee. Bag-pipes, while structurally suited for the drone, require a special finger technique for the grace notes and appogiatura to make them produce the dance rhythms.

The instrument inherently suitable for all types of folk-dancing is the fiddle. The bite of the bow on the string gives the impulse—the vibrating string itself

H

providing the continuous sustaining element. It has gradually ousted the pipes, and become the accepted form of folk-dance instrument. The fiddlers have inherited the traditional airs from the pipers and much of the pipe technique of slurs and grace notes. Right up to the end of last century intinerant dance fiddlers who could 'call' the dances were active throughout the British Isles. They shared an extensive repertory of folk-music and enjoyed a prestige similar to that of the minstrels in the Middle Ages. Surviving folk-fiddlers employ a technique very different from the violin-playing of the modern concert artist. It is probable that the fiddle itself was developed, independently of the violin, out of an older instrument, the Crwth, and that fiddle-technique owes part at least of its character to the older instrument. The fiddler plays with a shortened bow much more over his instrument, holding the body of his instrument against his shoulder or chest, rather than under his chin. As he has to support his instrument wholly with his hand, he plays in the first position without altering his grip. This leaves his head free to watch his dancers and to call the dance figures. In order to secure the element of continuity, he allows the bow to strike an open string, producing a drone effect not unlike that of the bagpipes. In the Hardanger region of Norway, a special type of fiddle is still constructed which has a supplementary set of strings lying beneath the usual four-fingered strings. These additional strings vibrate sympathetically, so that the drone effect is continually produced even when bowing a single string.

The folk-fiddlers in the past picked up their repertory of folk-tunes by oral tradition, but some of them made a practice of keeping a manuscript music-book in which they wrote down their melodies, or enough of each tune to remind them of the whole. These manuscript fiddle-books constitute a valuable repository for the collector and student of folk-music. Thomas Hardy, the novelist, who was a notable dance fiddler in his native Dorset, not only inherited his grandfather's book of fiddle tunes, but he made one of his own. In this book, now preserved in Dorchester museum, is reflected the popular folk-dances of the period and the melodies which were locally favoured. The old manuscript collections, unfortunately, do not reveal the style and manner of fiddling. For that one must seek a living exponent of this old fiddle school. They may still be found fairly plentifully in parts of Ireland and Scotland, including Orkney and Shetland. In England they are not so plentiful, but even so, one finds them playing for the traditional Sword Dances and Country Dances in Northumberland, and at many village dances in Cumberland. William Wells, the blind fiddler of the traditional Morris Dance team at Bampton, belongs to this old school. He is over eighty, and now finds it hard to tune his instrument. In spite of the imperfections, his playing has that unmistakable stimulating quality that makes you want to jump out of your chair and jig about the floor. He has an individual habit of amplifying his drone effects by humming the tune to himself as he plays. When this peculiar behaviour was pointed out to him by a B.B.C. technician who wanted to secure a clear recording, and who regarded the chanting as a gloss upon the fiddle-music, Wells replied that he had always hummed and that was the beauty of his playing!

In more recent times the fiddle itself is being supplanted by 'squeeze-boxes' which are easier to learn, and which keep themselves in tune. The melodeon, accordion and concertina family has established itself as a most efficient form of all-round dance instrument. Of these, the English concertina is undoubtedly the most compact and flexible. It can play in any key and has as wide a range as a violin. The Anglo-German type of concertina, sometimes called the 'Improved English', differs in its key-board arrangement, and plays a different note according to whether you push or pull. It is easier to learn than the orthodox English concertina, but the player has a very limited choice of keys. The melodeon, and its more elaborate cousin, the button accordion, is also built on the push-pull principle, but is as limited in key choice as the German concertina. It possesses, however, the immense advantage of an independent bass accompaniment which enables the player to provide a compelling rhythm. To the instinctive player the push-pull principle presents no difficulty whatever. The modern piano accordion, while it does not suffer from the restriction to certain keys, lacks the impelling drive of the push-pull instrument. Players of these metal reed instruments for the most part learn their tunes by heart, and pick up points of technique from each other. They study the playing of the virtuosi and extend their repertory by listening to gramophone records and the radio. Records of traditional folk-dance players are not very numerous, but at least they are more accessible than the players themselves. The gramophone enables the folk-dance player to learn his folk-music by the old method of picking up his tunes by ear.

No matter what instrument is employed, sooner or later the player realises that playing for dancing is an art in itself. Dance-music exercises an instant appeal. The pulsations of sound are answered directly by pulsations of movement. The music is felt rather than heard, and the body, behaving like a musical instrument itself, visibly responds. This is the effect when the process of response is unselfconscious. Unfortunately, such a response can only be expected to be found in young children and in that rare bird, the 'natural dancer'. What the natural dancer wants is an added incentive to his instinct to throb and to quiver. To provide that the music must have a vivid life of its own. The mere outline of a melody just does not suffice. It must be brought to life so that its infection gets under the dancers' skin. To accomplish this, the player must go through the process of dancing himself. Even if he need not actually bounce up and down, he must feel what it is like to be dancing, and relate his playing to that feeling. He must develop a lively imagination and a ready sympathy. Many musicians who try to play for folk-dancing start off with a completely wrong picture in their minds. They believe they are helping the dancers by emphasising the metrical beat. The reader will appreciate that this is just the part of the rhythmical cycle which can be left to look after itself. What the dancer wants to hear is a surge of sound which carries him along on the crest of its wave. This requirement in the music is difficult to indicate by means of conventional musical notation. In fact, some of the implications normal to musical notation have to be ignored for dance-playing. William Kimber, the Headington Morris man, him-

self a brilliant exponent of the Anglo-German type of
concertina, tells would-be dance-players to 'Play to
your dancers—the music is for them not for an
audience'.

Just because folk-dance tunes are simple and built up
of short lengths, musicians are apt to look upon them
as elementary stuff, involving no problems of treatment.
In fact, within their small compass they are as ex-
quisitely complicated as any other product of nature.
One can play such tunes for fifty years and still discover
something quite fresh, or suddenly see them from a
new angle. However well worn, they never wear out.
They fulfil all the canons of art at their own level.
That is why certain tunes, like 'Hunt the Squirrel', can
survive unchanged for over three hundred years and
still sound as fresh as the day they were born. Any
player who will take the trouble to learn a folk-tune
by heart, and be prepared to woo it intimately and
master it, will find himself amply rewarded.

The dance-tunes fall into three main categories,
according to their 'times'. The tunes in 2/4 time are
classed as Reels: those in 6/8 and 9/8 as Jigs. The 4/4
tunes are the Hornpipes; these, when played with 'Scottish Snap', become Strathspeys. Some famous dance-
airs may be found in all three forms, and many tunes
are readily convertible from one form to another.

The Morris Dance-tunes comprise all three types, but
the hornpipe is the commonest. In many of the Cotswold Morris dances the quick steps are suddenly
changed into great leaps or 'capers', and the tunes have
to change, too. This Morris 'caper-music', slowed to
the pace of a great soaring leap, has a majestic quality
possessed by no other dance-music.

The dance-tunes have been derived from a variety of sources, but the majority are modified song airs. Some offer no clue to their original source. Others again are comparatively recent. The itinerant dance-players acquired their collection of tunes ready-made from an earlier generation, adding new samples which they considered valuable to their stock-in-trade. Through the agency of folk-singers and fiddlers, traditional tunes have travelled far and wide. In the process of transmission they frequently altered, and some were even re-moulded to the point of becoming unidentifiable. It was not until the folk-players began the practice of writing out their tunes that these had the chance to settle down and become fixtures. While they lived solely in the minds and fingers of the players they were fluid things, subject to wide ranges of variation. It is this process of evolution and change within the minds and hearts of simple people which eventually gives the unmistakable imprint of 'folk' to a melody. When they have moulded their music to suit their taste they keep what they like best and discard the rest. Just how a tune begins, whether composed consciously or unconsciously, is of little importance in this matter of 'folk' character. Popular songs of any age were raw material for your traditional player. Folk-songs and ballads from the earliest times have been transformed into dance-airs.

The evolution of folk-tunes can be studied both in the live music of the country fiddlers playing for the Morris and Sword Dances, and in the preserved music in the various editions of printed collections of dance-tunes. The country fiddler of to-day has a stock-in-trade which includes Irish song and dance-tunes, Scots' reels, American mountain songs, Victorian music-hall songs and English folk-dance airs. He manages to give each of his varied collection a personal and individual twist, and he would be astonished if he realised what a hotch-potch his repertory actually is. The most interesting bunch of English folk-dance airs which have been gathered by the country fiddlers are the Cotswold Morris Dance-tunes. Some of these have been broadcast by gramophone and radio to such an extent that nearly everyone must know them by this time. When Mr. Percy Grainger first heard William Kimber's Morris tunes, he realised at once that here was music of an unusual kind with vitality and freshness. When he 'dished' them up for the piano, even he did not realise what smash hits they were going to be. 'Country Gardens' quickly went round the world, and 'Shepherd's Hey' was not far behind. Errand-boys have been prone to whistle them ever since. While it is not disputed that Grainger's arrangements were ingenious and effective, it was the tunes themselves that made the appeal. The traditional musician from whom they were obtained has ever since had to listen on the wireless to his home-made Oxfordshire music labelled as the work of Percy Grainger. It is not, of course, Percy Grainger's fault that the words 'arranged by' are so frequently omitted.

Sir Harry Lauder has a shrewd ear and instinct for a folk-tune. He has always managed to pick a good one in the way Robert Burns did for fitting his topical verses. The origins of certain of Kimber's Oxfordshire Morris tunes cannot be traced, but these have the appearance of being very old. Some can be tracked down to a definite origin, while others again may be followed into the distant past until a point is reached when investigation stops for lack of further record. 'Shepherd's Hey', for instance, is clearly a very ancient dance-tune, but it seems to have no traceable ancestry. 'Haste to the Wedding', another Morris Dance of Kimber's, as well as a popular Country dance-tune, is evolved from a song written by a James Hook about one hundred and fifty years ago, called 'Rural Felicity', but he may, like Harry Lauder, have been just writing new words to an old home-made tune. 'Hunting the Squirrel', another Kimber Morris tune, has its broken history traceable through the printed collections of Country Dances for two hundred years, until a point is reached backward when it melts again into a remote background as a name for a country ritual. Ever since that tune first won its place in the fashionable dance-books of the 17th and 18th centuries, its folk form must have continued in its country habitat. Cecil Sharp noted several variants of it when he was collecting Sword Dances in Yorkshire. The Sword dancers' name for it is 'The Wife of Dallowgill', or 'The Lass of Coverdill'. The air is mentioned by this name in the Calling-on song of the Kirkby Malzeard Sword Dance and in the Ampleforth Sword Play. It is also the tune for the Ampleforth Dance, and this version is the most impressive of all the variants. It may be nearer the original than the printed version of two hundred and fifty years ago.

There is a tendency on the part of the scholars to regard the folk-tunes collected in this century as mere degenerate versions of finer tunes composed sometime in the past. They find it hard to believe that a tune can be enhanced by the innate art of an uneducated peasant. A study of the history of folk-tunes indicates that degeneration and enhancement were processes that went on side by side in the stream of oral transmission. One individual player will beautify and embellish any tune he plays, while another will, as readily, wipe the bloom off every tune he touches. There is an excellent example of enhancement in William Wells' version of 'The Nutting Girl'. This rather unlovely country song has a dull little plaintive tune that I find singularly lacking in attraction. Yet it must have enjoyed a wide popularity, for it often turned up when the folk-song collectors were at work early in the century. Wells completely dresses this plain figure in a pattern of ornamentation, prinked out with grace notes and other embellishments. The result is a creation of singular beauty. Hundreds of dancers have revelled in the pleasure of dancing 'The Nutting Girl' Jig to Wells' version of the tune, but few of these dancers would ever connect his dance-air with the commonplace song out of which it is created. No doubt many of the Morris tunes have been carved out of mediocre songs; in fact, we know the detailed history of quite a number. Somehow their contact with the Morris Dance itself, and the art of the country musicians who gave the Morris 'flavour' to any tune they adopted, have transfigured the original into something infinitely more valuable. Vaughan Williams, the composer who has done more to restore and make popular the folk-song and the folk-dance tune than any other English musician, has always regarded the Morris Dance, with the tunes which the players have created for it, as a monumental contribution to the art of music.

X

How 'The Folk' Dance

THE first impression of almost all English folk-dance steps is that they look very ordinary. The practised dancers appear to be moving about in a business-like way with too important a job in hand to allow room for airs and graces. The job absorbs their whole attention, and yet there is an underlying current of excitement that now and then comes to the surface and communicates itself directly to the onlooker. One does not need to know anything about dance technique to appreciate that there is an economy and certainty about the action that betrays skill, but just wherein the skill lies is not at all obvious. One can study an expert team many times and still fail to put a finger on the secret. In this chapter I am going to try to describe some of the details of dance movement in the hope that my verbal picture will help the reader to see the interplay of forces behind dance action. Some of the illustrations in this book may help but no photographic 'still' can be expected to give an adequate impression of movement. I will choose certain samples of the different types of dance with the characteristic steps and gestures that belong to them.

I said above that *almost* all the steps look very ordinary. The reservation is made on account of one or two examples that are so queer as to rouse wonder at their very strangeness. In observing the Padstow Hobby Horse Dance, even when you have got over the first shock of its primitive savagery, and the sinister black and red decoration of the mask, there is something outlandish in the dance movements themselves. They get their weird character from the manipulation of the hooped frame-work and the tarred canvas skirt that flaps and swirls as the horse careers about the street. By contrast, the ambling steps of the Minehead Horse are dull and phlegmatic, but he has only to execute a neat pirouette and spin his great boat-like body for one's heart to miss a beat in expectancy of some devilish caper to come.

The Horn Dance at Abbots Bromley casts its spell over the onlooker not merely by the uncanny animal-like behaviour of the horn bearers. The slow jog-trot rhythm of the ten dancers who wind in Indian file with measured and unhurried step has its own hypnotic power. These animal-men trot in a manner that is dictated by the burden of the antlers pressing on their shoulders. The characteristic steps of the Cotswold Morris Dance are no doubt the outcome of the ceremonial regalia and dress and of the bells which are worn on the feet or legs. The steps look queer at first sight. With further acquaintance, they seem as natural and as functional as the flight of birds. If you are to discover the key to the dance action you must study it with great care. It is only too easy to take in the general appearance without grasping the reality behind it.

The Royton Morris men who dance in wooden clogs perform all their actions with an off-hand nonchalance. The basic figure is called 'Step-up', which is simply three walking steps forward, swinging the free leg upward by the weight of the clog. While they do that, they whiffle their slings, and the eye of the onlooker, intrigued by the perfect co-ordination of slinging and stepping, is apt to see wrongly and to register mere 'stills'. Only young children could capture immediately that rhythmical co-ordination. The ordinary adult will overdo it, putting into his interpretation of the movement much that is not in the original, simply because his attention has been caught by some by-products of rhythm and vitality. When you are accustomed to watch a Morris Dance, you derive the same solid satisfaction that you get from seeing a passing cart-horse and hearing the inevitable clip-clop. Sometimes when the Royton dancers surge forward in their 'Step-up', they catapult back again in a 'polka' to their places. This 'polka' or double-step is the ubiquitous step in all 'Morris'. It begins with a quick lift of the body in order to jump on both feet, one foot falling a fraction ahead of the other to make a 'ti-tum'. The sequence ti-tum, step-step, i.e. the double-step, once mastered will carry you through all the men's dances of the Midlands and North and many of the social Country Dances too. It can be, and is, danced to tunes of even and uneven time. The actual placing of the feet is subject to considerable variation according to the context of the dance. But the Morris dancers have many other steps beside the double-step. There is a wide range of back-steps, their differences depending on whether the weight of the body is on both feet or only on one: if on one, whether or no the supporting foot is given a twist, whether the free foot is swung out or swung across, placed behind or at the side, and so on.

These different types of back-step have a variety of names, some of which are delightfully descriptive. Hop-back-step, cross-back-step, shuffle-back-step, hockle-back-step, and wide-back-step. These are all variants of the 'single', which can always be substituted with a walking step by a flagging member of the team without destroying the rhythm or throwing the rest of the dancers into confusion.

In the Cotswold and Lancashire Morris the handkerchief or sling may be spun or twisted three times to match the ti-tum, two, three, of the stepping. This is a very common co-ordination. But in many of the Cotswold Dances the handkerchiefs are given a lift on each bar of music as the dancers jump off the ground—the handkerchiefs falling as the feet execute the steps. It is this fluttering of the handkerchiefs that gives a bird-like character to the dance movements and an emphasis to the ripples of rhythm expressed through the arms and hands. The actual hand movements have no doubt evolved out of the need to make something flutter and wave. When the hand movements are performed without the kerchiefs, as they are in the solo jigs danced by the Bampton Morris men, they would look spasmodic and rather meaningless if the onlooker did not automatically imagine the kerchief in the jig-dancer's hands. Comparison with the ritual dances of other people, such as the Veddas in India, suggest that the dancers may have earlier carried and waved green leaves or branches.

If the hand movements have grown out of the need to make leaves or kerchiefs dance, undoubtedly the range of steps has grown out of the need to make the bells jingle. The whole leg is worked from the hip joint, using the undulation through thigh, knee and ankle to shake the bells before the dancer, after his jump, alights on to the ground with a conclusive ring. This shiver of the free leg, coupled with the snap or snatch of the 'polka' rhythm, is the most characteristic feature of the Morris step and the one so difficult for the amateur to capture correctly. This shiver of the leg would now be an essential element of style even without the bells. Probably the shiver of the free leg in some of the old Court dances is derived from the much older rituals in which bells were once worn. But the particular steps in the Cotswold Morris Dances that arouse the most interest and curiosity are the Galleys and Capers. The Galley or Hook-leg is a leap on to one foot: while the dancer hops once on this supporting foot the lower part of the free leg rapidly describes an inward circle with the toe pointing downward. In England the Galley only figures in certain of the Cotswold Morris Dances. It doesn't occur in the Lancashire Dances, but the Basque dancers in Spain use a strikingly similar step. In fact, the only difference noticeable in the Basque Galley is that the circling foot describes an outward instead of an inward turn. In this it closely resembles that once popular Music Hall step known as the 'American Twist'. The 'cuts' in the Highland step dances may have a common origin with the 'Hook-leg' of the Morris. One can hazard guesses at the origin of this significant gesture, but they can only be guesses. It may once have been symbolic of the brushing aside of evil forces. There is confirmation of this in the whiffling sword of the Rusalii dancer, who also stands on tiptoe and circles or 'cuts' the free leg as he cleaves the air with his blade.

Whatever actual interpretation is put upon the Hook-leg, I have no doubt that it was once invested with specific ritual significance. To see six Morris men surging round in a circle suddenly spin each on his own axis, while six legs simultaneously twist in the air, is more than merely spectacular. It shakes one by its unexpectedness and awakens some primitive love of the incongruous in our nature. I have often watched its effect on different spectators. Smiles will wreathe some faces, but these smiles are not necessarily derisive. Young girls are liable to shriek at every Galley, controlling themselves between times but spontaneously bursting out again at the sight of the twisting legs. I should hesitate to class that reaction as mere hysteria.

Your old Morris dancer, to demonstrate how well he has kept his suppleness, will throw you a Galley as a greeting. I have seen the late Harry Taylor of Longborough (Glos.) at the age of 75 greet a fellow dancer coming down the village street with a couple of Galleys, one on either leg, which many a young athlete would give much to emulate. But the young dancers come into their own when it is a matter of cutting Capers. The Full Caper, or Split-jump, of the Cotswold Morris calls for a fine physique as well as a developed sense of rhythm. After three quick jumps, made off both feet, kept closely crossed and neatly tucked under the body, the Morris man leaps high in the air, throwing up his arms and handkerchiefs, while his legs flash apart—one foot forward and one back—as he remains suspended for an instant in the air. He lands as lightly as thistledown and promptly dances his three quick cross-steps before he is up again in the air for another Kick-jump. There are many varieties of Caper, but all share in the

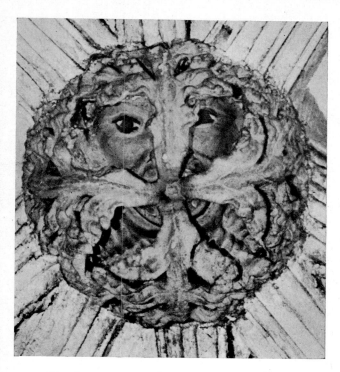

19. The Green Man, 14th Century boss from the Lady
Chapel, Ely Cathedral.

20. A Country Dance, performed to the English pipe and tabor.

change from the low-level jigging hop to the clear leap in the air. The simple Caper, or leap from foot to foot with a wave of the arms is used very often to bring a dance to its conclusion with the 'Caper-out'.

The Caper is a good example of a folk-dance step that is not quite what it looks at first sight. The impression given to all but the keen observer is that of a muscular spring made off the foot, thrusting the body into the air. The step in reality is exactly the opposite of that: the dancer lifting himself up into the air so that he can drop lightly on to a resilient foot. The succession of simple Capers is a series of rebounds with the energy concentrated on to the downward movement directly comparable to patting or stotting an india-rubber ball. A good Caper should neither involve nor appear to involve upward muscular effort. Normally the simple Capers are danced to the same rhythm of music as the jigging steps, but as the in-between hops are omitted, the Capers require only half the number of footfalls. For the more complex Capers, i.e. Kick-jumps and Double-Capers, the music undergoes the same kind of modification and is broadened out to half time. This does not slow the onward march of the dance itself but serves to give time for the successive leaps, and turns the dancing of quick shivering steps into a series of sweeping majestic movements. Just to hear the sudden change to 'Caper music' is a thrilling experience in itself. The origin of the leaping Caper is not so obscure as that of the Galley. An ancient Cretan hymn speaks of the youths 'leaping for full jars'. The Morris Caper is a symbol of bourgeoning and of the onset of Spring itself.

Although England no longer maintains a distinctive

I

class of peasantry, or 'folk', comparable with the peasantry of Central and Eastern Europe, the English traditional dancer of to-day has inherited a manner of dancing which bears the authentic stamp of his peasant ancestry. They can take their turn in an International Festival, dancing their own native dances alongside peasant dancers from other lands and not seem out of keeping. If the English dancers appear more conscious of their art, that is because they are the more conscious artists. Among the peasant lands of Eastern Europe— in the Balkans, for instance—the folk-dancing still smacks more of ritual than of art. But even in England the traditional dancers, conscious artists though they now are, cannot hide the ritual nature and origin of their dance-forms. It is this trace of ritual ceremony that gives to all traditional folk-dancing its distinctive style, and indicates that the dancers are in the direct line of their peasant forbears.

The English traditional teams differ from each other in local background: some are miners, some land-workers, and others industrial workers. Yet they all show a common trait in their manner of dancing. They become impersonal. Their dance demeanour is grave and dignified, but their faces are serene, as of minds turned inward. This is not an affectation. Rather is it the effect of the dance upon its performers. They are readily subject to its spell. Such a manner of dancing cannot be captured except by the process of surrendering to the spell. It cannot convincingly be imitated. To the non-traditional folk-dancer—the revivalist—the process of mastering a Sword or Morris Dance is a process of gradually surrendering himself to the form until the dance can exercise its spell upon him. When individual self drops into the background, the impersonal style begins to show. The greatest compliment that can be paid to a 'revivalist' team of folk-dancers is to class their dancing as 'almost traditional'. This would signify that the team had graduated through the teething stage of self-expression to the level of 'group impression', if I may invent a phrase to describe something very old but now rather rare. The anthropologists have their scientific label for this 'group impression', and they speak of 'participation mystique'—a rather elaborate description of a group of people who have been taken out of themselves into a larger unity. But the scientific term implies rather more than this. In the process of losing oneself in the dance the group find each other, not just as unselfconscious persons, but as tuned components, like the successive notes of a melody. This dance-group relationship is, in essence, musical, in the sense that a working harmony has been established. This unselfconscious absorption is reflected in the performances of folk-dancers in all parts of Europe. It seems to have escaped most observers who have referred to rustic custom in literature. Possibly the book-writers of the past have been too conscious of their own more sophisticated culture to see in the simple country customs anything more than the sad reflection of a lowly place in the social scale. They are prone to assume that peasant dances must be the degenerate relics of clever inventions of some bygone aristocracy. But at least the social dances must have exhibited a cheerful and high-hearted attitude to life, for it was the processions and rounds of May Day that made England merry. It was these that the Elizabethans brought into Court and promoted over the Norman French dances into the proud place held by the Country Dance for nearly three hundred years. The literary references to these 'new' domestic dances of Tudor and Stuart days certainly conjure up scenes of cheerful lightheartedness. The earliest descriptions of the English Country Dance performed by the gentry indicate unaffected movements, characterised by a gay simplicity. For the English Country Dance the word 'merry' has always been the apt and natural expression.

If the ritual Morris and Sword teams perform with a grave absorption, the attendant characters are unhibited and lively enough. The 'Squire' may fool around with the 'Betty', and the Hobby prance down the middle of the set, while the team of dancers weave their figures with that air of complete detachment that marks the ritual dance. If this air of detachment is inherited by the traditional dancers, it can also be developed by the process of team dancing over a number of years. This has been proved by the 'revivalist' teams of Morris and Sword dancers created by the English Folk Dance and Song Society. But what happens when a member of a highly skilled team drops out and creates a vacancy—how can his place be filled?

The traditional method is simply to put a young dancer into the vacant place. Brought up with the local customs throughout childhood, the recruit heedlessly absorbs the images of the dances and the style. He learns them by watching, by taking in the process through his eyes, as a boy learns to handle a boat or a car. Although he is not consciously aware of the details, nevertheless his body is, and instinctively he dove-tails his movements into those of the team and soon learns to play the appropriate part. Thus the tradition is captured right from the start. No other method can do that. Naturally it can only be fully effective when there is already a team, endowed with the necessary attributes, and when the man chosen to fill the vacancy has lived close alongside, and frequently witnessed, the annual dance celebration. When Cecil Sharp undertook his conscious revival, he had to start virtually from scratch, and build up a technique and create a style by an analysis of his own impressions. Because the folk-dance is instinctive and natural, any analysis of the manner and style of dancing is extremely difficult to make. The experience of thirty-five years of trial and error has proved that the traditional method of plunging the recruit into the side is still far and away the best, and so far as practical conditions permit, it should be followed.

To capture the technical action and style of a traditional team by a process of analysis requires much careful and patient observation. Even the most careful observation cannot ensure a replica, for different people see different aspects of the same thing. It is useless to try and act the part of the traditional dancer. That would only lead to a clownish caricature. One has to learn what actions are significant and what are the important elements of style to graft into one's own movements. In spite of these difficulties, the picture of a dance-movement received as a whole is much more effective than any detailed analysis, however clear and apparently accurate. The general style being acquired, the details seem to fall into place as a natural consequence.

While we can dispose of the new dance recruit very

simply in the case of the men's team dances merely by creating a vacancy in the team, it will take the recruit some considerable practice, with sweat and tears, before he is tuned to the pitch of losing himself in the combined operation.

In the case of the social dances, absorption is naturally more expeditious. In the simplest community dances the novice is assimilated quickly and vanishes into the throng without trace. But even if the novice in the country dance learns to get about, to take the initiative and to control his partner, it may take him quite a long time to acquire a style. The style of the traditional country dancers varies with locality, although they are all alike in their impersonal attitude and in using the body to control and direct the movement. Some traditional dancers always seem to keep the arms tight to the sides, but, in fact, they are held lightly, and are merely prevented from swinging about unduly. The legs and feet are kept well under the body, the whole bearing is compact, and the movement over the surface of the floor smooth and progressive. There is a noticeable absence of effort, and no appreciable spring or thrust off the surface of the floor. With developing skill there is a marked economy of effort, and the good dancer gives the impression that he never gets tired or hot, and that he could keep going continuously all night long.

Where the social folk-dance survives as a local tradition, as it does in the Border countries, there is no call for revivalist treatment. While players are available to provide the dance-music, the local dances will continue to give their undying pleasure. Where the local tradition has been lost, revivalist methods can and do reinstate the old forms and fit them for the use of the new generations. But the process of restoring a lost tradition has not proved an easy task with the folk-dance in England. The first attempts at reviving the country dance were marred by the choice of dances too difficult for popular use. Even with the simplest community and square dances, and with the help of Calling and infectious dance-music, there is a barrier to rhythmic response which is difficult to overcome. This barrier lies within the nature of sophisticated modern man, and it raises problems of such interest that I propose to devote a further chapter to its consideration.

XI

The Barrier of Self

IT has been the lot of many dance enthusiasts to invite
to a folk-dance gathering a reluctant acquaintance, who
insists that he only intends to look on. The general
atmosphere of social enjoyment and the rhythm of the
music gradually overcome his reluctance and he agrees
to join in a dance on the assurance that he will find it
quite simple. To his surprise, he finds it both simple
and delightful, once he has got over his initial shyness.
He is then ready to try anything and may even have
to be restrained from embarking upon dances beyond
his capacity. The simple dance that led to his undoing
was one that required no physical skill beyond that of
walking across a room, and his shyness and fear of
making a fool of himself were banished by the attention
he had to pay to the needs of his partner and of the
other dancers in the set. If he is allowed to join in a
less simple dance that deflects his attention back on to
himself, because of some physical movement outside
his day to day experience, then he will become self-
conscious, awkward and be only too ready to revert to
the part of onlooker. The discomfort he experienced
was due to his consciousness of being unable to conform,
rather than to the inability itself. In fact, he is per-
fectly able to conform, but he has, like most adults,
allowed his innate bodily skill to languish and has con-

ceived a false picture of dancing and of his own physical actions. The misconceptions that otherwise intelligent people have about dancing are almost unbelievable, and it is these distortions, coupled with quaint ideas of the organic functioning of their limbs and bodies that make any self-conscious approach to folk-dancing so unsatisfactory. Picture the Bampton Morris men with their swinging legs, their upflung arms and the rippling handkerchiefs transmitting the pulsations from their surging bodies. There is nothing tangible to get hold of—for the mind. Yet give a child two or three years' old a pair of handkerchiefs to wave and it will dance the Morris. You might think that you could take the place of one of the six Bampton men. I've tried to myself. You feel convinced you could dance just like them if only you could let yourself go, but there is a barrier standing in the way—the barrier of oneself as seen through the conscious mind. The mind of the educated adult of to-day has become so used to the role of know-all, and to interpreting messages from the senses intended for other destinations, that it assumes its interpretations to be infallible. Moreover, not content with trying to analyse rhythmical movement as the eye sees it, the mind actually interferes with the body's instinctive attempts to respond in the way it feels most fitting. This conflict is most acute among intellectuals and accounts for the jerky and spasmodic nature of their first essays in dancing. Given its chance, the body will gradually reveal its latent ability to dance, but the conscious mind is no easy adversary to overcome. Until it becomes bored or can be side-tracked, it will cramp and stifle the body's natural attempt to behave as an organism.

Throughout the history of the folk-dance revival in England, various methods have been tried to solve this problem. The prevailing tendency has been to make the first presentation less and less analytical and technical. Now, the different forms of dance are presented as a dance elaboration of walking, and the first stage aims at building on the natural rhythm of each individual's personal walk, however restricted and limited that may be. Many of the Morris Dance steps are embroidered walking steps. In the Abram Circle Dance, for instance, the step throughout is one that can be performed at sight by anyone who allows the action of walking to expand. Yet my experience of this very simple Morris Dance, taught to hundreds of dancers of different ages, has revealed that the vast majority of adults find the movement difficult. The instinctive dancers, and of course young children, can perform it at sight, and with the correct style from the start. The very fact that young children can naturally perform this primitive dance and adults cannot, clearly indicates that the function of rhythmic bodily co-ordination pre-exists in the human animal, and that this atrophies in the processes of growing-up and getting educated. For the folk-dances of the past to have any meaning and value to the people of the present, this atrophied bodily competence must first be restored. The best restoratives are probably the folk-dances themselves, but most of these, simple though they be, are still too elaborate to be used as corrective medicine for severe cases. Only a few very elementary forms are effective, in that they possess the capacity to side-step self-consciousness, to prime the drying-up springs of rhythm, and to recreate the organic creature.

The restoration of a sensibility for movement, and of the sense of rhythm, is heavily handicapped by the warped conceptions held of dancing itself. There is a prevailing idea that music in relation to movement is only useful to measure the action and to keep it in time. An experiment to demonstrate the impact of dance-music upon adults produces quite surprising results. If a group is asked to walk naturally and heedlessly, and is then invited to respond to a simple dance-tune, the immediate effect is an unnatural gait. The members of the group consciously try to regulate their movements to the beats they hear. After a brief, confused period, they will be marching in time. But the movements, which were easy and unaffected while they were heedless, will have become stilted and affected. The result will be different if the attention of each walker can be diverted so that the response to the music is, as nearly as possible, unconscious. For instance, if one of the group acts as leader and gets the others to follow in a chain and keep in accord with his rhythm before the dance-tune is played, the change-over can be accomplished almost unnoticed. Then as one or two become conscious that they are in fact walking in rhythm, and in accord with the music, they will fall out of rhythm again and the process will have to be repeated from scratch. Only by a gradual process of re-education can the mind be placated. The simpler the dance, and the more obvious the nature of the movement, the sooner is the mind satisfied to leave such childish matters in the care of the body. Once the body has demonstrated its ability to cope with simple rhythmical movements, it is in a stronger position to reassure the mind that other movements of this category can safely be left to it. Another method of deflecting the self-conscious mind is to tire it out. Constant repetition of a very simple movement bores the intellect—to the great benefit of physical fluency. When the body has to grapple with more complicated dance actions, then the mind can be provided in advance with a competing interest upon which to fasten. This requirement is fairly easy to satisfy in the social dance, where the individual dancer can concentrate personal interest and conscious concern upon the needs of his partner. In the ritual folk-dances this concentration of interest must be upon the requirements of the team as a whole.

In both forms, social and ritual, the dancer has eventually to set up a working relationship between body and mind whereby the mind changes from the role of busybody to that of collaborator, becoming content to second and implement the impulses and motions first expressed by the body. While 'thinking it out' interferes with rhythmical action, nevertheless there is a form of mental activity which promotes and heightens it—namely the use of the imagination. Even if we may not walk gracefully, we most of us walk quite naturally so long as we do *not* think it out. Once we think of how we walk, we become self-conscious, and are plunged into a discordance. But while we remain unconscious of our walking, the style of action varies according to our mood; it expresses our hidden purpose, our internal environment. If we are careworn our walking declares it. If we are carefree our walk may become so impregnated with rhythm as to create music, a by-product of our good spirits, in the form of whistling or singing. Such a buoyant walk, expressive of general enjoyment, makes a satisfactory basis for dancing. If we cannot create this basis by conscious effort, we can often capture it by vivid imagining. Once the buoyant walk acquires a positive rhythmical character, the feeling of it can be registered as a dance technique, which in turn can be made the basis of subsequent dance skill.* The dance walk derives its energy from the upward and forward impulse of the body. The actual footfall or step is a result of the subsequent relaxation to the pull of gravity. Between each step, and particularly during that moment of upward rise, is the expressive zone, the build-up of energy (or tension), which is followed by its expenditure (or relaxation), the two together forming a pulsation. The alternation of rise and fall in a series of pulsations constitutes a wave action, and this exhibits itself outwardly as rhythm. The appearance of surge between each step is not dependant on the height of the rise, but on a delaying factor before the step which may be described as 'reluctance'. This 'reluctance' can be varied in degree by the dancer, delaying the footfall, and producing an effect recognisably expressive and rhythmical.

So far I have fought shy of defining the meaning of the word 'rhythm'. Nearly everyone imparts his or her own shade of meaning to it. I am at present using it to mean 'the appearance of flow', which is a quite literal translation of the original Greek word. 'Appearance of flow' presupposes a ripple, or a waviness, not mere smoothness, and it is just this waviness that dis-

* I must warn the reader at this point that I am getting involved in the consideration of physical rhythm, the discussion of which is difficult.

tinguishes a rhythmical walk from the utility pedestrian movement which has no emotional content to express. When the self-conscious mind is side-tracked, and with it the mechanical conception of a mere succession of steps and the regular measures these beat out, then the physical body, which is by nature and evolution physically skilled, seizes hungrily upon the expressive zones between the footfalls and turns them into a series of pulses. The living body itself functions in terms of continuous vibration and undulation. The mind, finding difficulty in grasping anything so complex, is only too ready to impose its ill-conceived picture of a discontinuous sequence of positions and attitudes.

We can now turn back with some relief to the appearance of the actions of the Morris dancer. As he leaps and hops we can trace the undulations spreading from his body through his legs down to his feet, and out through his arms to his finger-tips and handkerchiefs. A slow-motion picture would suggest an analogy to those sea-creatures that progress by an alternating expansion and contraction of the whole of their bodily substance. It is on this kind of pulsating picture that the mind should feed if it wants to play a helpful part in the field of instinctive bodily action. It must be provided with images which bear a close relation to organic functioning.

With the right mental picture of rhythmical movement, the dancer is stimulated to fall naturally into spontaneously co-ordinated movements that have all the appearance of natural grace. At the beginning of the century 'graceful' implied artificiality, but the word has now recovered some of its original prestige. To move gracefully is to move harmoniously as a fit and healthy animal does, so that the head, limbs and trunk fall into an organic pattern. A condition of grace in dancing can only be reached if the physical and mental faculties have arrived at a working partnership, and if the whole surface of the creature is being fully employed for expressive purposes. The young have this faculty, but tend to lose it rapidly as they grow up and are educated. There is one other faculty of the young which they tend to lose as they grow up, but which, if it can be retained into maturity, is a priceless asset. That is the faculty of being able to take in through the eye, in one sweeping embrace, the general contour and rhythm of any physical action. Children have so strong a visual faculty that they can imitate with equal facility the gestures of the grown-up, and the antics of their own kind. This imitative faculty, which children share with monkeys, gradually atrophies through lack of use. It serves us on occasion, but we cannot depend on it. The golfing novice who bases his first shot merely upon the dazzling example of a skilled player is often surprisingly successful. His first shot may be a winner, but, alas, his next and many more after are clownish efforts compared with that glorious fluke. He has started to think, and once self-analysis begins he must sacrifice his pleasure and his leisure to the ministrations of a coach, who has then to build up consciously in the teeth of incredible misconceptions, a bodily co-ordination which the novice found intuitively for his first imitative stroke. The folk-dance novice should learn to take in images in one gulp. He must avoid trying to analyse his visual picture into little pieces. The fluent gestures, the leg shakes and quivers, are not to be analysed without completely changing their character. The earnest student who says, 'I must know what I have to do before I can do it', is insulting his instincts and his long line of physically competent ancestors. He is declaring that he does not want to dance at all—in fact, that he wants to do something quite different. Even the physically literate and most expert dancers would not be so presumptuous as to claim that they knew exactly all that they did when they danced. The body 'knows', certainly, but its 'knowing' is a very different knowing from the knowing of the mind.

*   *   *   *

Once the initiate has experienced the feeling and ex-hilaration of rhythm and can overcome self-conscious-ness he need not encounter any great difficulty. He is well on the way to graduating as a 'fool', in the folk-dance sense of that word which I have tried to explain elsewhere. Further progress lies in a growing sensitive-ness and responsiveness, and in the give and take of the team dance. Once the dancer has been 'tuned' each further experience sharpens his skill and broadens his technique. One sphere of dance-action where im-provement comes rapidly is in the dancer's relation to the surface of the ground. He develops the 'act of touch', the art of being able to land lightly as a feather or to put all his mass behind an emphatic stamp, with every kind of gradation in between. Another field of increasing skill is in speed of relaxation. Most dancers can relax at the speed of a leisurely walk, but as soon as the tempo increases they stiffen and press off the ground in a series of spasmodic jerks. It is the capacity for rapid relaxation that distinguishes the first-class step-dancer from his less nimble fellow. I am here using the word 'relaxation' in a specific sense—namely, as a part of the cycle of rhythmical pulsation. The other part of the cycle is usually given the label 'tension', but this is an undesirable word to bandy about among dancers. To many 'tension' means only a condition of stress, and 'relaxation' one of complete collapse. I prefer, instead of 'tension', to use the word 'anacrusis'—a Greek word meaning 'before the crest', or leading up to a crisis, as a wave piles up before the crest tumbles over and breaks.

In folk-dancing the important moments and movements happen during the period of the anacrusis. In the Morris Dance this is the moment of the flying kerchief and the swinging leg, with its pad of jingling bells strapped to the shin. When these ring they do so not only on the main beats. In between the primary beats are the secondary shakes and shivers which give that sense of vitality to all primitive dance movements.

A third and extremely important part of dance-skill upon which much else depends is the carriage or poise of the body. The ambition of the dancing body is to keep the weight off the feet. Quick undulations and relaxations are possible only if the dancer is lightly poised. That very heavy part of the body, the head, has to be balanced so that it does not bias the dancer in any particular direction. There is a knack in balancing the head so that it is readily helpful and yet does not absorb too much energy in being kept in place. Nearly every civilised person requires some adjustment in the carriage of the head. Once this is adjusted, the body tends to fall into a straight line from head to toes. The feet should normally fall directly underneath the line

K

of the head and the long axis of the body. The up-
and-down equilibrium in itself is not difficult to attain,
but a much more important function of dance-carriage
is that of making the dancer light on his feet. Your
rationalist will, of course, say this is not possible:
that if a dancer weighs 12 stone, he weighs 12 stone.
Your real dancer, however, knows better. Whatever
he may weigh in fact, he can decrease in fancy and in
relativity. The buoyant carriage, known as 'balon'
in ballet technique, does, quite definitely, lend wings
that lift the dancer through the air and over the ground.
Even if the conception is partly psychological, it is none
the less effective. With the head we cannot do better
than to balance it delicately upon the neck, but the
arms can be encouraged to carry their own weight.
Lifting them away from the sides of the body gives a
definite feeling of buoyancy as well as of increased
freedom. The whole upper part of the trunk can be
lifted up from the pelvis like an egg out of an egg-cup.
Using the 'elevated' carriage, the dancer gradually becomes physically aware of the air as a medium. He finds
it offers some degree of tangible support like a swimmer
floating on the water the non-swimmer distrusts.
There is another aspect of this uplifted carriage which
encourages the dancer to feel less earth-bound, and that
is the capacity to reach out expectantly, and to make
contact receptively. On this attitude of expectancy,
or receptiveness, is built the magic of the team dance,
with its demand for a developed faculty for give and
take. To take part in a team dance is a very liberal
education. It teaches the dancer how to combine a
high degree of individual freedom with the necessary
give and take of a live society. The selfish individualist

has no place here, for until his self-centredness is tempered with appreciation of the needs of others, his presence is merely irrelevant. But if there is no place in the team dance for the egotist, it is equally unsuitable for the subservient. Many learned commentators upon the folk-dance have fallen into the error of assuming that participation implies the complete surrender of the individual. This error would be admitted readily if such critics could and would join in the dance themselves. An habitual team dancer might find it hard to define how much he is free and how much he is tied. He would unhesitatingly claim that he is not only free, but that much initiative is required of him by the rest of the team. His ties, too, are not fetters, but part of a harness designed to let him pull his weight. He would say they hang lightly on him like an old coat.

Dance posture is not invariably an upright one. In the English Sword Dances the dancers are often in anything but an upright position—sometimes, in fact, being almost on all fours. Even in that bent-up position they have to continue to step expressively, and move rhythmically and generally further the requirements of the team. Their poise is always dynamic. When carriage and receptiveness have been developed to the point of confidence, then communication can pass from individuals throughout the group, quite unimpeded. The power that is generated in a Sword Dance is a source of constant surprise and pleasure to the dancers. It is far beyond the sum total of the individuals involved. How it manages to multiply itself is one of the many mysteries of rhythm.

But further discussion of the folk-dancers' art would weary all but the specialist, and it is not for him that this book is intended. Already I am sensible that much of this chapter may be incomprehensible to the non-dancer. That is the trouble with writing about dancing. Until the reader has actually experienced the feeling of a dance movement, description and discussion cut little ice. Those who have felt the experience have no need for any argument. To those who have not, I can only suggest that it is never too late to give the folk-dance a trial. It deserves their patronage, for is it not a part of their national heritage? The English dance-forms, with their native traditional tunes, will strike a chord in every English breast if they are given their chance. The dances and folk airs are not just out-of-date anachronisms. They are old friends wanting to be recognised. I believe that there never has been a time in England's history when the people stood in more need of refreshment at the springs of their own traditions and of the new life that these can give.

XII

Two Morris Dance Tunes

THE two examples of Cotswold Morris Dances are re-produced from Morris tunes arranged by Butterworth and Cecil Sharp by permission of Novello & Co. Limited. George Butterworth, until his death in action in 1916, was Cecil Sharp's close collaborator.

The tunes, Bonny Green and Leap Frog, both undergo the broadening process associated with the Full Capers, and both are set dances for six men. Bonny Green, which is one of the Bucknell (Oxfordshire) dances, probably gets its name from an old song air with words referring to 'Bonny Green Garters', the name by which the tune is known in other Cotswold Morris traditions. Leap Frog is named from the frog-hop caper which occurs in the dance and which is believed to have had fertility significance. Both dance tunes are probably very old. They bear the authentic stamp of the Cotswold Morris Dance and their like is not be to found anywhere else in Britain.

I hope the reader to whom they are unfamiliar will whistle and sing them, or will carry the book to a piano and try them over several times.

Bonny Green

HANDKERCHIEF DANCE

Collected and arranged by Cecil J. Sharp and George Butterworth

Leap Frog

HANDKERCHIEF DANCE

Collected and arranged by Cecil J. Sharp and George Butterworth

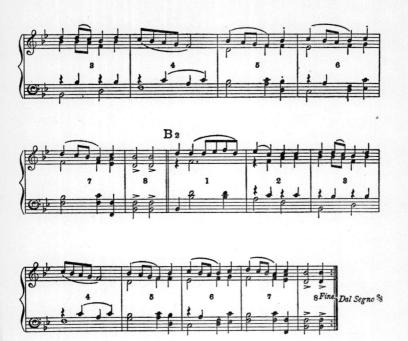

Bibliography

ALFORD, Violet, and Rodney GALLOP. *The Traditional Dance*. Methuen, 1935.

BASKERVILL, C. R. *The Elizabethan Jig*. Univ. of Chicago Press, 1929. Bibliographical notes and citations. Textual specimens of stage jigs.

BRAND, John. *Popular Antiquities:* 1777 and various editions later.

CHAMBERS, Sir E. K. *The English Folk Play*. Clarendon Press, 1933. Bibliography. Textual examples.

English Literature at the close of the Middle Ages. Clarendon Press, 1945. Bibliography.

The Mediaeval Stage (two volumes). Clarendon Press, 1903. Bibliography.

FRAZER, Sir J. G. *The Golden Bough* (eight volumes). Macmillan. Or one-volume Abridgement, 1923.

The Scapegoat (being Vol. VI of *The Golden Bough*). Macmillan, 1913.

GRAHAM, John. *Lancashire and Cheshire Morris Dances*. Curwen, 1911.

HAMBLY, W. D. *Tribal Dancing and Social Development*. Witherby, 1926. Bibliography.

HARRISON, Jane. *Themis: The Social Origins of Greek Drama*. Cambridge Univ. Press, 1912. Bibliography.

Ancient Art and Ritual. Home Univ. Library. 1913. Bibliography.

HOOKE, S. H. *The Labyrinth*. (Further studies, by various hands, in the relation between Myth and Ritual in the Ancient World.) S.P.C.K., 1935.

KARPELES, Maud. *The Lancashire Morris*. E.F.D.S. 1930.

LAYARD, John. *The Stone Men of Malekula*. Chatto & Windus. 1942.

LEVY, G. R. *The Gate of Horn*. Faber & Faber, 1948. Index of Authorities.

MURRAY, Margaret. *The God of the Witches*. Sampson Low, n.d.

SACHS, Curt. *A World History of the Dance*. Translated and abridged from the original German by Bessie Schonberg. Allen and Unwin, 1938. Bibliography. Illustrations from contemporary sources.

SHARP, Cecil J. *The Dance*. (An historical survey of dancing in Europe.) Halton, Truscott Smith, 1924. Illustrations showing the dance from earliest times, selected by Paul Oppe.

SHARP, Cecil J., and others. *The Country Dance Book:* 6 parts published between 1909 and 1922. *Part I:* English Traditional Dances. *Parts II, III, IV, VI:* English Country Dances transcribed from Playford's *Dancing Master,* 1651–1728. *Part V:* The Kentucky Running Set. Novello.

The Morris Book: 5 parts published between 1909 and 1913. Novello.

The Sword Dances of Northern England: 3 parts published between 1909 and 1913. Novello.

STRANGWAYS, A. H. Fox, and Maud KARPELES. *The Life of Cecil Sharp*. O.U.P., 1933.

TIDDY, R. J. E. *The Mummers' Play*. Clarendon Press, 1923.

WELSFORD, Enid. *The Court Masque*. O.U.P., 1927. Bibliography.

The Fool—His Social and Literary History. Faber & Faber, 1935. Bibliography.

WHISTLER, Laurence. *The English Festivals*. Heinemann, 1947. Bibliography.

WILLIAMS, Iolo A. *England Folk Song and Dance*. Longmans, 1935.

Readers should also consult *The Folk Dance Journal* (1927–31), and *The Journal of the English Folk Dance and Song Society* (both obtainable from the E.F.D. & S.S.), which contain many articles of the ritual and social dances of England and Europe.

Index